CONTENTS

1

Published in 2015 by New Vista Publications

Part of Reflective Learning-International

Overton Business Centre

Maisemore

Gloucester

GL2 8HR

England

www.rl-international.com

Authors: Sarah Lee, Martin Dixon and Tony Ghaye

Cover Design: Shaun Taylor Photography. www.shauntaylorphotography.co.uk

Book Design and Formatting: Tony Ghaye

Printed and bound in England by Book Printing UK, www.bookprintinguk.com

INTRODUCTION – LEARNING FROM EXPERIENCE

This book is written for students and coaches-in-practice who are passionate and committed to improving what they are doing in the field of sports coaching. It draws upon the latest thinking from applied positive psychology. In this book we take the view that great coaches need to be acutely self-aware and reflect on their practice in order to develop, adjust, refine and improve what they are doing. To many involved in sports coaching the term reflection simply implies *'thinking about what you have done'*. This is a good starting point and will undoubtedly lead to some self-awareness. But in the world of sport much more than thinking about what you've done is needed if we are to improve what we do, whilst at the same time appreciating what we have achieved. This book aims to describe and explain how you can reflect and get the best from this learning process in order to become more consciously aware of your coaching actions and how to improve your performance and, in turn, that of others you work with.

From time to time, throughout this book, you will see some shaded reflection boxes (see below). We add these to the text so that you can constantly practice and get into the habit of reflecting on action. You can simply mull them over.

> **Reflection:**
>
> Why did Zinedine Zidane, on a balmy night that was to be both the pinnacle of his career and his swan-song, suddenly implode, head-butting an opponent in the 2006 World Cup Final?

At the heart of this book is the notion of improving performance – essentially your performance. So it starts with you, your feelings, thoughts and actions, and the consequences (or result) of your actions on others. It's not easy to talk about **your performance**, as performance is a big word that captures many things. So, right at the start of this book try to sort out the following in your mind.

Reflective activity:

What do you think is the difference between:

(a) PERFORMING?
(b) Your PERFORMANCE?

Try to keep a reflective diary/notebook, as you read through this book. In it write a sentence that sets out the difference between these two terms, that you currently have in your mind. A starting thought might be that one word might be more associated with action in-the-moment. The other might be more to do with your record of achievement.

We want to encourage you to begin to think about your performance as an athlete and/or coach? Here are some reflections by Jonathan Edwards (Britain's greatest triple-jumper) on the way he, and others, saw his performance.

After reading this, what does it say about **(a) performing. (b) performance**?

"I think I'm quite understated, so probably people don't realise the extent of the drive. For example Simon Barnes wrote in Sydney that I looked like a geography teacher and the most unlikely of Olympic champions. But Michael Johnson understood when he did a retirement tribute piece for me for BBC's Sports Personality of the Year, he talked about my mildness off the track but said that I was like an animal when I competed. It was interesting that Michael saw that

side of me. That this was something that came alive in competition. In fact, if I was winning a competition I would often get bored, slightly disinterested and go through the motions. But if someone went past me, I'd change in a heartbeat and become a completely different creature. So I guess I'd say I was very driven, but it's not particularly obvious." (Gogarty & Williamson, 2009)

Fundamentally this thin book is written as a practical guide to help you as students and/or coaches learn through **positive reflection** on what you do, so you can improve the quality of your coaching practice. This book is based on the notion that reflective practices help us understand the links between what we feel and think and what we do. In sport, understandably, a lot of attention is given to **performance outcomes**. That's often talked about as winning or losing and sometimes less about how you performed or played. In other words if you 'win ugly' that's ok, as long as you win!

Reflective activity:

(a) Think about a sport that you play or coach. Make a list of what you feel are the THREE top performance outcomes in your sport, at the level you play or engage in coaching.

(b) Then think a little deeper. Try to think of ONE good example of: (i) A performance outcome that YOU set for yourself. (ii) A performance outcome that is set from OUTSIDE. In other words set FOR you by someone else. State clearly who this 'someone else' is.

It is very important to understand how reflection is linked to action. To improve your action, you need to reflect critically and positively on your performance. So action and reflection need each other (see Figure 1). Figure 1 looks deceptively simple doesn't it?

Figure 1. Reflection linked with action

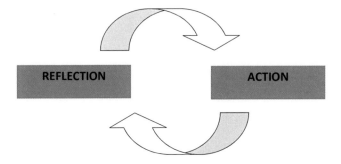

As you read through this book, we want you to get a clear message that to improve your performance you have to choose to reflect on something worthwhile or **significant**. You can't reflect on everything. You have to be selective.

So right at the start we invite you to think about this by trying to positively respond to the four reflective questions shown below. In answering these questions you can think about (a) Your **character** – the kind of person you are (b) Your **performance** – what you do and how you interact with others. These two areas will help you to build a picture of who you are, as a coach, and how you operate within your specific performance environment. It's a start point to improving your coaching awareness. If we are not aware of how we perform, we have little chance of improving it!

As you have a go at answering these four questions, try to be alive to what you are feeling and what you are thinking as you do so. The reason why we say this is because each of these questions is about YOU. They are inviting you to think carefully and deeply. In answering them they require you to examine how you **feel.** This means you are having to use your emotions. You also have to put something of yourself onto the page. This is called **self-disclosure**. So this requires some honesty. There is no virtue in deluding yourself. Have a go at these questions. They are not easy ones! So take your time.

Reflective activity:

Choose one significant aspect of your coaching practice. In order to 'get even better' at it:

1. What do you feel you need to **START DOING?**
2. What do you feel you need to **STOP DOING?**
3. What do you feel you need to **DO MORE OF?**
4. What do you feel you need to **DO LESS OF?**

In your notebook, draw up a table like Table 1. Write down your responses in the appropriate sections. You need to decide how often you complete this Table. Our suggestion is at least once per week. Then find someone you trust and respect to talk about what you've written. Don't forget to spend time discussing what ACTION/S might follow the learning you are making!

Table 1. Being the best I can be

Being the best I can be	
STATEMENTS	MY ANSWERS
1. What I need to START DOING	
2. What I need to STOP DOING	
3. What I need to do MORE OF	
4. What I need to do LESS OF	

You shouldn't be surprised if you got stuck on the first question because it may have required you to make a **choice** from a number of possible actions. It also may have required you to think about your personal **priorities**. Not easy! If you got stuck on the 2nd question, again don't be surprised or give up. This is another tough one. It may have got you to think about a **problem** you may have in your coaching, or a strategy you need to use in order to get rid of a coaching **weakness**. It's about what you should quit doing!

And what about question three? In trying to answer this you may have been reflecting on something about yourself (your character) or something you were doing (your performance) that wasn't quite 'right' or at the level you were hoping to achieve. So we asked this question to get you to think about what you need to do **more of**. To actually do this may require you to have a mental attitude of not going easy on yourself! Not cruising, but pushing and challenging yourself to be better than you are now. The last question may also have been a tough one. So what are you prepared to let go of?

We suggest that you come back to your answers after about a week and certainly after you've read through this book. Then take another look at what you wrote to these four questions. Basically we are asking you to think about what really matters to you as a coach and how you feel you can practically improve (not just change) what you do and how you get the best out of the athletes that you work with.

> **Reflection:**
>
> Coaching should focus on future possibilities, not just on past mistakes. What do you think?

Many people think that reflection is an 'armchair' activity. That you do it after an event or training session. You literally do it sitting down, alone, while walking the dog, or as you prepare a meal later in the day. You mull things over in your head. You work things out for yourself as you go over and over incidents, having a kind of private conversation with yourself. Doing this is important. So keep doing it. But it's not the only way to begin to link reflection and action in order to improve what you do.

Additionally in this book we invite you to think about how **data** can help you focus your reflections and help you think about particular aspects of your own, or someone else's performance. Of course data can be gathered in many ways and be in different forms. For example it can be in written, pictorial, graphical or numerical forms. Sometimes people refer to data as being **qualitative** (e.g., descriptions and interpretations) or **quantitative** (e.g., numbers and statistical significance). **ALL** data about performance needs careful analysis and interpretation. There is almost always more than one interpretation to be made of the same data! And be aware of the fact that some people in sport favour some kinds of data (statistics) over others (personal experiences).

Reflective activity:

Look at the Table of data below. On the day when Messi wins his 91st cap (in the Rio World Cup 2014) he draw level with Diego Maradona, the last Argentian No. 10 to reach the semi-final of a World Cup. So comparisons are inevitable and understandable.

(a) What do you conclude from this table of data?

	Lionel Messi	Diego Maradona
International Caps	91	91
International Goals	42	34
World Cup appearances	13	19
World Cup goals	5	8

Now take a look at the data below. There are two tables of Formula 1 data. The first is about the performance of Lewis Hamilton, a GB Formula 1 racing driver in his first 9 races in 2014.

Reflective activity:

(a) What are THREE important things this data tells you?

Table 2. Hamilton's First 9 Race Results 2014

2014 season – the first 9 race results

Race	Finish	Points
Australia	Retired	0
Malaysia	1st	25
Bahrain	1st	25
China	1st	25
Spain	1st	25
Monaco	2nd	18
Canada	Retired	0
Austria	2nd	18
Britain	1st	25

Now take a look at Table 3 below. It shows comparative data. It is Hamilton's performance alongside the performance of his Mercedes team co-driver, Nico Rosberg.

Reflective activity:

(a) State THREE questions this data raises in your mind. You may have to think again about Table 2 above to help you.

Table 3.   2014 F1 Driver Standings After 9 Races

2014 FIA Formula 1 Drivers' World Championship standings after 9 races

	Driver	Country	Team	Points
1	Nico Rosberg	Germany	Mercedes	165
2	Lewis Hamilton	GB	Mercedes	161

We have to reflect on something significant. And sometimes this 'something' can be puzzling, challenging and open to different interpretations. For example **'match stats'** can fall into this category. But as coaches we need to work with them and reflect on them. They form a vital part of a coach's 'tool box'.

Reflective activity:

Take a look at the match stats in Table 4 below. They are those of the match between Roger Federer and Novak Djokovic in the 2014 Wimbledon men's singles final.

(a) What do you conclude from these stats?
(b) How do you think Djokovic won?

Table 4. Match Statistics from 2014 Wimbledon Men's Singles Final

Novak Djokovic		Roger Federer
		Match time: 3 hrs 56 minutes
13	Aces	29
3	Double faults	5
62	1st serve %	69
73	1st serve win %	77
65	2nd serve win %	44
68	Winners	75
27	Unforced errors	29
4 of 15	Break points won	3 of 7

Sometimes data is not in number form, it can be in pictorial form. Pictures, both as video and in still formats can be strong triggers for reflection. They can bring back vivid memories and stimulate the emotions. There are many things you can do with pictorial images. It might be useful to find a trained performance analyst to help you use them. For example take a look at these two contrasting images of Novak Djokovic during his Wimbledon finals match.

Reflective activity:

1. What do you think is happening in this picture? It occurred in the 2nd set of a five set match?
2. What are the performance implications?
3. What thoughts (if any) do you think his coach may have?

Reflective activity:

After the match, Djokovic headed into the stands to celebrate with coach and former champion Boris Becker.

1. Find out the role Becker plays in 'team Djokovic'.
2. What does this image suggest is the kind of relationship between the two champions?
3. Describe the best coach-athlete relationship you have experienced.

Sometimes a combination of data can be a powerful aid to reflection. Take a look at the example below.

Reflective activity:

1. What interpretation do you make of this aspect of Djokovic's performance (it's his 1st and 2nd serve return placement).
2. If you looked at this through the eyes of a tennis coach, what would you say to Djokovic in your post-match reflective conversation?

Djokovic's ability to produce high-class returns at crucial stages in the match was key to his victory. A clear tactic he used was to return to the Federer backhand. The second-serve return was where Djokovic was most dominant, (see Table 4 above) returning at an average speed of 68mph and winning 56% of those points. Federer returned Djokovic's second serve at an average speed of just 57mph and only won 35% of those points. With both players dominant on first serve, taking advantage of the second was vital.

The last thing we wish to raise in this INTRODUCTION to this book, is the importance of reflecting on your performance through **conversation**. Reflective conversations can be the catalyst for progress, change and good working relationships between you and your athlete/s. Lane[4] a performance management company has developed a model for what it calls a **high performance conversation.** The model has four parts.

1. **Contracting**
    This comprises 3Ps:
    a. *Practicalities* of the conversation – the timings, logistics, roles and responsibilities;
    b. *Professional* – being clear about the objectives and purpose of a meeting;
    c. *Psychology* - the hopes, fears and expectations surrounding a conversation.

2. **Awareness**
This is the way you demonstrate awareness of the values, emotions, knowledge and experience held by yourself and those you are coaching.

3. **Authenticity**
This is all about your self-awareness and appreciation of the impact you will have on the other person in the conversation and them on you. You need to try to be yourself.

4. **Trust**
Lane[4] believe that there are four parts to trust. It is the sum of;

a. *Credibility* – your expertise and how you appear to others,
b. *Reliability* – your dependability and consistency,
c. *Intimacy* – your ability to connect with the other person.

They go on to suggest that these three things should be divided by the coaches' *self-Interest.* That is how much they put their needs ahead of others!

Reflection:

If winning is all in the mind, what do you think of golfer Sergio Garcia's comment that he would rather never win a major tournament than suffer years of unhappiness pursuing that goal?

A summary:

1. Reflection is more than just 'thinking about what you have done'. It is learning from these reflections and using this learning to adjust, change and improve your future action.

2. Performing and performance are two different but related actions. It's important to know the difference.

3. Improving your practice requires you to become self-aware. Without this personal characteristic you will struggle to improve anything!

4. Positive reflection is a process where you critically analyse both your strengths and your limitations.

5. You need to reflect on something important and significant in your practice. So you need to be clear about what you choose to reflect upon and why.

6. When you reflect on your practice, try to be as honest as you can, with yourself and others. There is no point kidding yourself. There is little to be gained by self-delusion!

7. Think about the kind of data you need in order to focus your attention and stimulate your interest in improving some aspect of your practice. This data might be words, sounds, pictures, graphs, numbers and any combination of these. This data is often called qualitative and quantitative.

8. Most practice improvements involve having a conversation. There are limits to learning alone. So try to have a (high performance) conversation with a trusted, critical but supportive friend/colleague.

PART ONE

BEING THE BEST YOU CAN BE

This book isn't based on the idea that you can be anyone you want to be. It's based on an idea that you can be a LOT more of who you are already! Put in another way, this book is about how to get (even) better at things you are already good at. To use a phrase from the field of applied positive psychology, it's about trying to *be the best that you can be*. This phrase means that you try to improve what you do, as often as you can. Please note that we use the word improve, not just to change your practice/s. There is a big difference between *change* and *improvement*. More about this later.

```
What kind of coach are you?
```

In order to make a start with this, it's important that you get as good as you can at self-reflection. Have a look at the statements below. Quickly complete them. Don't over think your answers because what comes to mind first is important. Answer them by thinking about: (a) yourself as a coach or (b) yourself as an athlete.

Reflective activity:

- ➤ I would never ....
- ➤ I hate it when ....
- ➤ I get a lot of satisfaction when ....
- ➤ I don't know why they make me ....
- ➤ I would be better if ....
- ➤ The best way to do things in the future is ....

When you feel you are at your best, what kind of coach are you? Are you an enthusiastic coach? A charismatic coach? A technically competent coach? An ultra-competitive coach? Would you say that you were patient, supportive, a good listener or perceptive? An expert? Some or all of these? Maybe something else?

Reflective activity:

1. Choose a coaching colleague, peer, or someone who knows you professionally.
2. Think about how you would tell them your **'Me at my Best'** story. What will you say?
3. Take up to 5 minutes to tell your colleague this story. Set the scene at the start. The middle will expand and add details for your colleague and the end will wrap things up.
4. Ask your partner to listen out for the strengths you described as you told this best moment story. Then invite them to tell you what they thought about what they heard.
5. Then swap and listen to your colleague's story.
6. Have a conversation about what you generally admired in each other's story.
7. What (if any) surprising things have you learned about your partner?
8. How did your colleague feel when you were talking about your strengths?
9. How did you feel when listening to your colleague's account?

10.What have you learned about developing and using a 'strengths vocabulary?'

Reflective activity:

So ...... what kind of coach are you? Write 50 words answering this question.

You may have described yourself in the best and most positive way. Why not? For example, you may have said that you are the kind of coach that has a commitment to work hard for your athletes, so they can be the best they can be. You may be the first on the training ground and the last off. Or, for example, you may have answered the question differently. You may have described yourself as the kind of coach that delivers 'stimulating, engaging and technically sound' sessions.

Reflective activity:

When you are at your best and positively 'engaging' your athletes in a coaching session, what are you normally:

  (a) Feeling?
  (b) Thinking?

If you find this difficult to answer, it usually means that you need to think about developing your self-awareness more. In other words, becoming more aware of your feelings and thoughts and how far you are able to talk about them. This can be hard.

Here is another thought. You may have described yourself as an 'inclusive coach.' Being inclusive means *adapting and modifying your coaching practices* and activities to ensure every participant, regardless of age, gender, ability level, disability and ethnic background has the opportunity to participate if they choose to. Good coaches adapt and modify aspects of their coaching and create an environment that caters for individual needs and allows everyone to take part.

Arguably some of the qualities and skills (performance and character strengths) of an 'inclusive coach' are:

- **Patience:** Recognising that some participants will take longer to develop skills or make progress than others.
- **Respect:** Acknowledging difference and treating all participants as individuals.
- **Adaptability:** Having a flexible approach to coaching and communication that recognises individual differences.
- **Organisation:** Recognising the importance of preparation and planning.
- **Safe practices:** Ensuring every session, whether with groups or individuals, is carried out with the participants' safety in mind.
- **Knowledge:** Utilising knowledge of coaching and training activities and how to modify/adapt them in order to maximise the potential of every participant.

Our reason for inviting you to reflect on what you regard as your positive qualities and strengths is this. The better able you are to recognise strengths within yourself, the more aware you will become at distinguishing, acknowledging and appreciating strengths in others. More about this later.

Adaptations and modifications are normally described as **CHANGES** to your practice. Fundamentally these changes can be of two kinds. (a) **Behaviour changes** (you do something differently) (b) **Changes in attitude and of mind** (you feel and think differently). In other words maybe you are more positive or more prepared to try out something new. If you regularly and systematically reflect on your coaching work, you may feel there are things you might need or want to change for next time. When you normally think about changing your practice, you probably do this because you want to get better at doing something. In other words the changes you make are *'intentional actions'*. You deliberately think about them and try to execute them.

Reflective activity:

Which of these three options do you feel is the key to being the best you can be .... AND WHY?

The ability to change your: (1) Coaching style and techniques (2) The way you communicate with different athletes (3) Attitude when things don't go according to plan?

Another way of looking at this is to see change as something to do with aspects of these four questions we asked you earlier:

(a) **STOPPING** something you currently do
(b) **STARTING** something you're not already doing
(c) Doing **MORE OF** something you already do
(d) Doing **LESS OF** something you already do.

But changing your behaviour and your attitudes isn't always easy and inevitably can take some time.

The acronym **'CHANGE IT'** may give you some more practical ideas to help you change your coaching to meet the individual needs of your athletes.

> ➤ **C**oaching style: e.g. demonstrations, or use of questions
> ➤ **H**ow: e.g. to score or win
> ➤ **A**rea: e.g. size, shape or surface of the playing environment
> ➤ **N**umber of participants involved in the activity
> ➤ **G**ame rules: e.g. number of bounces or passes
> ➤ **E**quipment: e.g. softer or larger balls, or lighter, smaller bats/racquets
> ➤ **I**nclusion — e.g. everyone has to touch the ball before the team can score
> ➤ **T**ime — e.g. 'How many ... in 30 seconds?'

Reflection:

If there was only one 'right' way of doing something, Fosbury would never have flopped and Bjorn Borg would never have won Wimbledon. Getting good at change helps you be the best you can be. What do you think?

It's good to be aware of the different tools and 'models' that can be used to help you focus on the changes you wish to make in your practice. The **GROW model** might be useful to consider.

Goal setting for the session (end goal, performance and process goal/s)
Reality checking on current knowledge, skill and motivation levels
Options and alternative courses of action you have built into your planning
What you will do, when, and why.

When you think about goal setting it may be helpful to follow the PURE advice. By this we mean make sure it is:

Positively stated

Understood by your athletes

Relevant

Ethical

Reflective activity:

The Olympic motto is, 'stronger, faster, higher'. But say you wanted to add a 4th word which is '*smarter*'.

   (1) Think about what smarter means to you. What aspects of your coaching might you change in order for you to coach smarter?

Another practical change tool is called **TREE** (shown in Figure 2). You can use **TREE** to help you to (a) plan for or to (b) reflect on some of the most significant (important) changes you made recently in your coaching.

Figure 2.   The TREE Tool

T	Your 'TEACHING' or coaching style
R	The 'RULES' and instructions you give
E	The playing or performance ENVIRONMENT
E	The EQUIPMENT you use

Reflective activity:

Have a go at using **TREE** in this activity.

You need to have TWO coaching sessions in mind. These should be linked sessions. One is where you delivered the first session of the series. Then after reflecting on it, you decide to make a/some change/s. The second session is where you try to execute these changes. So for example, after your first session, what (if any) *changes* did you make to your teaching or coaching style....... AND WHY?

1. What was the aim of the first coaching session?
2. After thinking about how it went, what CHANGE/S did you make?
3. Why did you make them?

What is performance?

There is much talk in sport about the difference between the outcome (result) and the performance. This talk is often linked to conversations about success and failure. Sometimes both the performance and outcome is good. In other words you win and win in style. At other times we hear the expression, 'to win ugly.' This might be linked, not so much with how you win, but simply winning in any way possible. Just doing what it takes to get a positive result.

This book is called, **IMPROVING PERFORMANCE: COACHING THROUGH POSITIVE REFLECTION AND ACTION**. We therefore have to ask (at least) two fundamental questions:

(1) What does really good **performance** in your sport look like?
(2) In what ways can you **improve** your own and others' performance?

Something that might help you with this notion of performance emerged from the UK Sport, post-2012 London Olympic, World Class Performance Conference. The on-going focus there was on medal success, and in Rio 2016, to be at least as competitive as Team GB was in 2012. It was argued that achieving this would require the development of an even stronger and more sustainable high performance system.

The theme for the 2012 World Class Performance Conference (WCPC) was *'calibration'*. This meant that those in elite sport wanted to take the opportunity to check, or rectify, their current position in order to successfully plan the future of their sport. Four areas of recalibration were identified. They were:

(1) The **SELF**
(2) Relationships
(3) Sustainable success
(4) Performance focus

All of the statements so far in this section are about performance.

In this thin book, we focus more on area (1). In writing it we believe that your vision of what or who you want to be is the greatest asset you have. Central to improvement in area (1) are your responses to four reflective questions, posed to all delegates who attended that WCPC (see below).

Reflective activity:

Think about your coaching practices over the last 6-12 months. Ask yourself:

(1) What have I learnt?
(2) What am I ready to leave behind?
(3) What's beginning to emerge?
(4) What's most important to me?

Write down the best example you can think of, when answering each question.
Try to find someone (e.g. a critical friend, colleague, peer etc.) and talk to them about your answers. How do they respond? What are you going to do with what they tell you?

What follows is a list of some of the things that we know affect performance. For example your level of self-confidence and your drive to achieve your personal performance goals. Some of these performance related things are;

> *Self-Awareness* – being aware of how you feel and your level of motivation, and an understanding of how your feelings impact on your personal (coaching) performance, attitudes and judgements.

> *Self-Confidence* – your ability to respect yourself and to find things to like about yourself and be confident in your skills, and to believe in your ability to perform as a coach, for example.

> *Self-Reliance* – your emotional power to be self-directed and take full responsibility for your performance and your ability to be self-reliant in making significant decisions.

> *Competitiveness* – the strength of your desire to strive for success by performing at your personal best.

- *Achievement Drive* – your desire to be the best that you can be.

- *Resilience* – your ability to cope effectively with major setbacks and disappointments in coaching and positively manage negative emotions.

- *Focus* – your ability to maintain an effective focus on what you're doing and avoid distractions.

- *Flexibility* – your ability to be 'agile' and adapt your thinking and actions in response to changing circumstances as well as your ability to "go with the flow" to maintain optimal performance.

- *Self-Control* –your ability to manage your emotions well, stay calm when under pressure, and your ability to manage shifting moods in your athletes so that everyone thinks clearly and acts appropriately.

- *Optimism* – your ability to sense opportunities even in the face of adversity and maintain an overall positive attitude through playing to your strengths.

Reflective activity:

After reading through this list of things that affect performance:

1. Sort them into two lists.

   - **List A** = those things you feel you currently do well, are satisfied with and which you regard as strengths.
   - **List B** = those things you feel you wish to prioritise for attention and do something about to change.

2. Look again at **List A**. Choose one thing from that list that you are MOST proud of and/or satisfied with. Is there anything you need to think about changing so that you can play to this strength even more often.

3. Pick one thing from **List A.** What is the best example of this from your practice?

Here is an example of an 'agile' and 'emotionally intelligent' elite coach. His name is Andy Banks who coached the diver Tom Daley. We interviewed Andy just before the London 2012 Olympics. At one point in the interview we were exploring the ways in which a coach might get the best out their athlete. For example knowing when to push and when not to. Knowing how important it is to use different personal qualities, in the right way and at the right time, so the athlete can be the best they can be. Here is an extract to illustrate this.

Question: *This dictator to facilitator role – when you say you do this, it looks like it's a smooth process, but I guess there are times when Tom doesn't want you to facilitate, he wants you to dictate?*

Andy Banks: Absolutely. He said that to me once when I'd tried to push that but it's a relationship and therefore there are times when it does and doesn't work. In his first International he'd just split the Chinese as a young kid [silver medal]. Moving into the next round I thought it might be worth a try so I said to him 'what do you want to do for your build up to your final?' He just looked at me and said 'I want you to tell me what to do and I'll go and do it like you always do'! It was fine, that wasn't an issue I just thought I'd see what the score was and he obviously wasn't ready at that point.

Whereas now, he's 17 now and he's quite a mature young man and we discuss stuff a lot more. I've been to the school to meet with his deputy head to discuss his A Levels and what he's gonna do with them, when he's gonna do his exams and how that fits into this year, how that fits into next year and how that fits into 2013 as an addendum. That's all well and good, I can help set that up, I can help make sure the right people are there, but at the end of the day the decision is his; 'if you want to do your a-Levels this year that's what you're gonna do, these are the pros and cons of doing that, this is what might happen if you do that, what do you think?' I think it's very much a case of yes we'll steer and nudge and I know what I would prefer and I'll tell him what I would prefer, but ultimately I'm not telling him what he's doing, he will make that decision himself and if he needs help with it then we'll get other people in, then we'll get the psychologist to come in and talk to him, or his teachers will talk to him. So he's getting as many inputs as possible. It's not just about me and him, it's about the team again to try and make sure he gets absolutely everything that he needs to make the value judgements and decisions that he needs to make, hopefully in the right way.

(Dixon, Lee & Ghaye, 2012, p. 344)

> **Reflective activity:**
>
> Which of the qualities that you put in your Lists A & B, can you find in the thoughts of Andy Banks?

Gathering evidence about performance

In trying to be the best you can be, we suggest it's important to understand that: (a) *changing* your practice and (b) *improving* your practice are two very different things. Simply put, making changes to your coaching, is about: (i) doing the same thing differently (ii) doing something different. The change/s may or may not lead to better performances and results. Sometimes when changes are made, for example in training routines, things can have a tendency to get worse before they get better. They can get worse for a while as your athletes learn new things and new ways of training. This is often referred to as the 'U' shaped performance curve.

Generally we can talk about two **types of evidence**: (a) **Primary** (this is first hand evidence, for example you saw it for yourself, and found it out for yourself (b) **Secondary** (this is evidence gathered from someone else and can be articles, books and video etc.). Evidence can also be represented in two **forms**. This is often called: (a) **Quantitative** (as numbers expressed in different ways such as graphs and statistics) (b) **Qualitative** (words, pictures, sounds etc.). There are also many **ways to gather** evidence. Again this generally falls into two broad categories: (a) **face-to-face** such as through interviews and focus groups (b) **at a distance** such as through a postal or on-line survey.

Gathering evidence is an *intentional activity*. It needs to be done with a clear purpose in mind. In other words you need to know what evidence might help you answer the question you are asking, the dip in performance you are trying to address or the success you are trying to replicate and sustain. Is your intention to find out more about why you lost your last match, how you might improve the motivation of certain players, how to involve more young people in physical activity, or how to take on and beat the best in the world?

It may be unwise to rely on only one kind of evidence such as numbers or personal testimonies. Sometimes it's better to combine different kinds of evidence and to learn from the different/same things they may be telling you. This technique is often called **method triangulation**. This might make your personal understandings more trustworthy, and what you say and do with others more believable. If you gather evidence for a particular reason you also need to be clear when it's the most appropriate **time** to do this. For example gathering evidence about performance at time-outs, half-times, immediately after a match or later, is often a crucial decision. And with the help of modern technologies, evidence can be gathered and analysed in 'real-time' (as it happens).

Evidence is something you use. For example it can be used to:

(a) **Describe** or illuminate something (e.g., the way a coach gives a motivational speech).

(b) **Explain** something (e.g., why an athlete ran faster and faster in the 100m heats, but ran slower in the final).

(c) **Justify** something (e.g., changing your golf swing because you want to have more control over how far you hit the ball and where you are placing it).

(d) **Predict** something (e.g., if as a coach you talk *at* athletes too much and use a command-and-control style, it's possible to predict that, over time, this might have a negative impact on athlete motivation and participation. Notice we use the word 'might!' Every athlete is different. Some may like being heavily directed and being told what to do. Others may react negatively to a harsh tone of voice and few opportunities to express themselves. Some argue that the end justifies the means. In other words, if you keep winning, it's worth the experiences of physical pain, emotional discomfort and occasional social embarrassment).

(e) See a **trend** or **pattern** (e.g., through video analysis of a team's football performances a trend might be seen with regard to why the opposition seems to get far too many shooting opportunities. By looking at incidents that seem to change the rhythmic flow of attacking and defending, trends or patterns of play might be spotted that lead to shooting opportunities. For example, what always seems to happen from a penetrating pass, a dribble, a change of pace?).

One way to begin to **gather evidence about performance** is to use the **SWOT tool**. This stands for strengths, weaknesses, opportunities and threats to performance. The table below provides an example of how a coach has used the SWOT tool to identify different aspects of the player's performance. The player's name is Poppy. You might like to think about how you could use this tool in your coaching.

Table 5. SWOT Analysis

Strengths	Weaknesses
Poppy is motivated to succeed in tennis and is motivated by winning tournaments and working towards being the best she can be.	When Poppy loses a match, this causes low confidence which makes her feel like that she is the worst player at the club. It takes time for her to bounce back.
Opportunities	**Threats**
Poppy has the opportunity to work herself into the rankings and hopefully be able to compete in higher ranked tournaments.	Poppy has a tendency to push herself too hard in training and in a match situation this could cause injury and stress which would set her back on her progression up the rankings and will also affect her confidence.

Reflective activity:

1. Study the four statements, made by the coach, about Poppy's performance. What actual evidence do you think he gathered to make such observations?

2. How far do you think the coach may regard what he calls his 'instinct, hunches and feelings he has about Poppy', as evidence?

3. What do you think the terms: (a) hard evidence and (b) soft evidence might mean?

If you are interested and committed to improving your coaching practices, we suggest that you need to understand two key ideas. They are: (a) the need for, and the ways you might gather **evidence** about your practices (as above) (b) the ways you can use evidence to understand the **impact** of your coaching on performance, results, personal and team goal attainment, motivation, athlete well-being and much more.

Reflective activity:

In the UK there is a drop-off in girls' participation in PE and sport when they reach their teens.

> What **evidence** could you gather to support or refute this suggestion?

Reflective activity:

What **evidence** would you gather if you wanted to better understand the relationship between adolescent sport participation and lifelong participation in physical activity?

Reflective activity:

What might be the **impact** on athletes' feelings, thoughts and performance if athletes were made to feel constantly unsure regarding their selection for the next match or event?

Impact is a tricky word as it means many things. There are different kinds of impact. For example there is the impact our actions have on other people's feelings, thoughts and behaviours. There is economic impact such as cutbacks in athlete funding or the closure of training facilities and so on. When coaches say they want to *make a difference*, what they usually mean is that they wish to have a positive impact on their athletes. This can mean they want them to feel positive, confident, train well, eat sensibly and perform to the best of their ability.

In a paper about coaching practices, Santos, Jones and Mesquita (2013) suggest that over the past decade, sports coaching has come to be described as a very complex and dynamic endeavour. They argue that practices are often *context-bound*. This means that what works in one place, with one group of athletes and on one day, may not always work in other places and with others. They go on to suggest a broadening of our view of coaches. For example away from them as transformatory and 'heroic' people to coaches doing the best they can with what they have (Bowes & Jones, 2006). Put another way. They suggest that it is limiting to see coaching as unproblematic and something that can be cleanly planned and executed. They suggest it's much more concerned with coaches managing ambiguity and uncertainty.

In earlier papers on coaching practices, Jones (2005) and Jones & Wallace (2006) develop the intriguing notion of *coaching as orchestration*. The metaphor of orchestration suggests guiding or steering, as opposed to smoothly and painlessly directing individuals, teams and squads as this can be a very complex social process. This idea of 'orchestration' presents coaches' actions as stage managing events, involving continuous decision making related to on-going observation, planning, reactions to contextual 'things going on' and learning from reflection-on-action. Orchestration then, was offered as a more realistic conceptualization of coaching in terms of providing practical guidance for coaches to make the most of what they are able to do and how they can do it (Santos, Jones and Mesquita, 2013).

Reflective activity:

What kinds of **evidence** might you gather to illustrate *'coaching as orchestration?'*

What are the potential **impacts** for your practice if you start to think of *'coaching as orchestration?'*

Learning from and through reflection on what you do, can only happen IF you try it and are prepared to be open-minded about what you might learn from it. There are many kinds of reflection and you can reflect in many ways. In this book we are trying to give you some experience of this. The purpose is to help you improve your performance. By the time you've got to the end of the book we hope you will understand yourself better, have a better idea of your strengths and how to play to them and how all this might help improve your performance.

In order to achieve this, the book is informed by the principles and processes of positive psychology. It's a relatively new branch of psychology and is to do with happiness, well-being and optimal functioning. From our perspective, positive psychology is far more than supporting performance enhancement. A key focus of this field is assisting individuals to be the best they possibly can be, whatever their 'performance' activity is. That's assisting you as an athlete, coach, sports manager and so on, to be the best you can be! Positive psychology helps us do this through the twin processes of: (a) *building positivity* (b) identifying, using and developing new *character and performance strengths.*

Reflective activity:

1. Think about one of your coaching sessions. Choose one that is significant to you because it was one where you experienced *positive feelings*. What feelings were these? Try to list and describe what you were doing at the time to feel this way.

2. What would you have to do to re-experience these feelings again in a future session?

In this part of the book, we invite you to think about *positivity as a strength.* Positivity, like strengths, means different things to different people. It can also be fragile and can easily slide into something else, like negativity, feeling down and even depression. It is possible to be a positive coach. But it depends on how you feel and think. Like all emotions, positive ones arise from the way you interpret ideas, actions and events as they unfold. The hope for everyone is that we do have the power to turn positivity on and off for yourself. Positivity is not looking at the world through rose tinted spectacles!

There are many views of positivity. The most common is that of having a *positive attitude.* This usually shows itself in what is said and in actions taken. It can also show itself in positive body language through hand gestures and facial expressions for example. It's easier to be positive and upbeat when things are going well, for example when an individual or team is winning. Being positive when things are going less well is altogether different. In situations like this a coach may have to draw upon a lot of self-belief, courage of their convictions and support from colleagues. Positivity is also linked with the way coaches attribute the reasons for the lack of success to things within or outside of their control.

Reflective activity:

Experiment with this. Turn your positivity **ON** right now. Ask yourself:

1. What's right about my current coaching circumstances?
2. What makes me lucky to be coaching this/these athlete/s?
3. What aspect of my current circumstances is something I really treasure and value?

Now turn this positivity **OFF**. Ask yourself these positivity-spoiling questions:

1. What's wrong with coaching this/these athlete/s, right now?
2. Why do I feel so fed up?
3. Who can I blame for this?

When we feel positive we generally feel happier, are more resilient and creative. We feel we have more energy and determination also. So it is important that you get into the habit of reflecting on how certain positive emotions affect how you think and what you do.

What follows are five positive emotions that play an important role in coaching and in performance. Try to make time to work your way through each one. Write down your responses in a notebook. Writing reflectively is a skill we suggest you need to develop. Keeping reflective notes (which is something more and more often seen being done by coaches observing matches) or even keeping a diary, can be very helpful. If you learn from your reflections, you give yourself a chance to get better at what you do. But if you do keep reflective notes try to; (a) write about something significant, however you define this (b) do it over a period of time. If you manage this you may give yourself a chance to see patterns emerge. Patterns of thinking and action. Patterns of feeling and expression. You could even share your notes with a colleague and use them as a catalyst for a reflective improvement conversation.

Reflective activity:

Positive emotion 1

<u>**JOY**</u>

1. What gives you most **JOY** when you coach?
2. What are the 'triggers' for this?
3. What can you realistically do to amplify this positive emotion?

Positive emotion 2

<u>**INTEREST**</u>

1. What generates feelings of **INTEREST** when you coach?
2. What are the 'triggers' for this?
3. What can you realistically do to amplify this positive emotion?

Reflective activity cont:

Positive emotion 3

PRIDE

1. What generates feelings of **PRIDE** when you are coaching?
2. What are the 'triggers' for this?
3. What can you realistically do to amplify this positive emotion?
4. When have you felt most proud of yourself and your achievements?

Positive emotion 4

INSPIRATION

1. What generates feelings of **INSPIRATION** when you are coaching?
2. What are the 'triggers' for this?
3. What can you realistically do to amplify this positive emotion?
4. When have you seen someone perform, or act, better than you ever imagined possible and feeling inspired by this?

Positive emotion 5

LOVE

1. What is it that you really LOVE about coaching?
2. What are the 'triggers' for this?
3. What can you realistically do to amplify this positive emotion?

What are your standout strengths?

How far do you know your strengths? Usually we struggle to list them. We often don't know how many we have. And sometimes we get embarrassed when invited to talk about them. However we are often acutely aware of our weaknesses. You might think of strengths as those skills and competencies you personally do best. Another definition is that they are things that you do better than everyone else.

When thinking about your strengths be prepared to experience some difficulty. Weaknesses often get more of our attention than our strengths. This is because many people are trapped into thinking that we learn most and make most improvement, when we address our problems and get rid of our weaknesses. In doing so they tend to ignore what can be learned from success. They tackle their problems and assume that all the good stuff can just look after itself. Where is the logic in this? We suggest that if, as coaches, we only focus on the thing we need to put right, on failures to execute and on problems, all we learn is more about problems. We learn very little about success. A strength-based approach to coaching balances this focus with one that looks carefully at success. It tries to understand the root causes of success and how to amplify this.

As a coach, you may feel one of your standout strengths is *authenticity*. In other words you present yourself in a genuine way to your athletes and wear your heart on your sleeve. You may feel that leadership is a strength, or being creative on the training ground or being aware of the motivations and feelings of each athlete. This is called being socially intelligent.

As you think about this notion of *standout strengths* you may wish to think about:

1. Physical strengths
2. Mental strengths (mental toughness, focus)
3. Emotional strengths (empathy, resilience)
4. Social strengths (approachable, good communicator)
5. Spiritual strengths (can build hope and belief and a sense of loyalty)

For a personal coaching activity to be a strength, you must obviously have some ability in it. And your success, however this is determined, is a great indicator of ability.

Reflective activity:

Another way of thinking about your strengths, especially if you are a practising coach, is to think about your:
   (a) Character strengths (e.g. honesty)
   (b) Performance strengths (e.g. determination)

1. Think of your best TWO examples of each kind of strength.
2. What are you doing when you normally use these strengths?
3. Try to think of an example when you need to COMBINE and use both character and performance strengths in your coaching.

Reflection:

There are no bad strengths, just the bad use of strengths.

What do you think?

We suggest that learning a common strengths language is a very important part of being the best you can be.

Reflective activity:

Find someone you trust and have a chat with them about what you are really good at. Think about the last 2-3 months. During this conversation you don't have to try to persuade this person, or gain their approval, or even ask for help. You are simply asking that they listen to you. That they be your audience for 10 minutes as you find the best way to describe one or two of your standout strengths. The whole chat may take longer if they ask questions! And questions are good so don't shy away from trying to answer them.

We say **'standout strengths'** because we are asking you to avoid a shopping list mentality. If you mention a specific strength, for example like 'being determined', 'explaining things clearly' or 'an ability to form great relationships', then think about an example which best illustrates this.

We are suggesting that having a conversation about this is a good idea because the chances are you are (still) not very good at talking about your strengths. But you may be very fluent when it comes to talking about your weaknesses!! But be prepared. A chat about strengths (and weaknesses) is fundamentally an emotional one. So think carefully about *what* you say and *how* you say it. Talking about emotions, perhaps with the exception of those associated with winning and losing (i.e. competition), are largely out of place in most workplaces. So if you struggle a bit with finding the 'right' language, this is perfectly normal. But again be honest.

Reflective activity:

Have a *'how can you help me'* conversation.

This is a totally different kind of reflective experience. Again you need to find a trusted friend or colleague. Set up a 'how can you help me' meeting. It could be with the same or a different person than before. The point of this conversation is for you to describe ONE of your standout strengths and then ask the other to suggest how you might use this strength more often and in particular circumstances. So you are reflecting on what you want MORE OF, not what you want to get rid of! So ....

(1) Pick one strength and ...
(2) Pick one performance outcome that could be affected by *a greater use of that strength.*
(3) Talk to your colleague/friend about this.

Keep the conversation practical. Think about exactly what you want to do differently, and how, when and by how much. If it helps, put some numbers to the improvements you want to make and a timeline. To do the activity (above) well, you need to identify exactly how and where each of your standout strengths helps you in your current role. You also need to think carefully about the missed opportunities you might be experiencing to use your strengths more often. The real challenge of this activity is to think about ways you can build your work/practice toward each strength. In summary, 'how can you play to your strengths a little more this week than you did last week?' This inevitably will take effort and determination.

Who is the best judge of your strengths?

In this book we are stressing how important it is to reflect on *both* your strengths and to work around your weaknesses. In this part of the book we want to urge you to focus on improving your performance, and learning, by focusing on your strengths, understanding what success means to you and others, understanding the root causes of successful action and then amplifying the positive aspects of it.

How far do you think you can be trusted to know exactly what you are good at? Learning how to identify, clarify and confirm your standout strengths is important in improving performance.

So we invite you to have a go at an activity called the 'reflected best-self?' Lord Sebastian Coe (2009) talked about the best-self in this way: *"Aiming for excellence is not so much about gratifying the ego (beating everyone else for the sake of it) as the desire to see how far you can get, how much you can do – to become the best you can be"* (p. 3). So the notion of the reflected best-self is an expansion of this. For all those involved in improving performance, reflecting on those moments when you felt that your best-self was brought to light, affirmed by others and put into practice, is an important part of developing a 'portrait' of who you are (and what you do) when at your personal best.

This activity is different from the ones you've already done in this book as it is not so much about YOUR feelings, thoughts and actions but about how OTHERS see you. Scary stuff! So at this point we are going beyond the 'Snow White' approach to reflective practice, which starts and ends with oneself looking into a mirror and asking, 'Mirror, mirror on the wall, who is the best (student, coach etc.) of them all?' The reflected best-self activity is **not** a response to the question, *"When I am at my best I ......"*, but a response to the question answered by others namely, *'When I see you at your best you ....* It is the things we do, or show others, when at our best and as perceived by others. Of course others' perceptions of us may not always be the 'truth' on the matter. So again you need to find a trusted friend or colleague. Please be aware that it can be uncomfortable to ask others, 'What do you think I'm best at?' Or 'what am I doing when you think I am being the best I can be?'

Reflective activity:

Choose a good friend or trusted colleague. Then ask yourself:

1. When I am at my best I ....

2. Now ask your friend or colleague:

   "When you see me at my best, what am I doing?"

3. Now compare your two responses. What are you learning?

Effective coaches are always playing to their strengths and developing new ones. Without an awareness of your strengths, and how to use them, it's almost impossible to coach effectively and be the best you can be. Different coaches coach in different ways. One of the things that effects this is their awareness of their strengths and how to use them.

Rath and Conchie (2008) talk about four general 'leadership' strengths. We suggest they are highly relevant to sports coaching. They are the strengths of:

i.   **EXECUTING** – Knowing how to make things happen.

ii. **INFLUENCING** – The ability to take charge, speak up and be heard.

iii. **RELATIONSHIP BUILDING** – Creating positive relationships based upon high performance principles and processes. (See the *'high performance conversation'* in the Introduction to this book).

iv. **STRATEGIC THINKING** – Absorbing and analysing information to make better decisions and reach your desired performance goals. In order to further develop your self-awareness around strengths, try completing the reflective activity below.

Reflective activity:

Think about your coaching over the last month. Focus on the positives. Think about the best examples from your practice that illustrate some/each of the following.

ACTIONS	My BEST PRACTICE EXAMPLES
Execution	
Influencing	
Relationship building	
Strategic thinking	

> What do you need to do to keep doing what you are best at? Make a short list and prioritise the items.

The Olympic motto – *Citius, Altius, Fortius* – is Latin for faster, higher, stronger. Given the unique demands of competing against the best in the world, it is imperative for athletes to go beyond physical and technical expertise, and to develop the psychological and emotional strengths to excel. Providing coaches with:

(a) the appropriate knowledge and skills, and

(b) athletes with the understanding of how to achieve their optimal state for competition, and then

(c) equipping them both with the psycho-emotional strengths to perform, are vital roles that psychologists, of one kind or another can play, to enable athletes and teams to effectively cope with pressure and achieve peak performance.

The English Institute of Sport state on their website (http://www.eis2win.co.uk/pages/Performance_Psychology.aspx) that the mind has a key role to play in sport. They state that what we think, and how we feel impacts on any sporting performance. They go on to say that a positive mindset during training keeps the athlete (and coach) focused on making the small improvements to enhance performance. A positive mindset during competition may make that 1% difference between achieving, or missing one's goals. So this begs two questions. (1) What does the 'positive' in the phrase a 'positive mindset' mean? (2) How can we enhance positivity?

Observation as a strength

Arguably at the heart of being a good reflective coach are good observation skills (Ghaye, 2011). Coaches need to be able to observe what is going on in the interactions that take place in the performance environment in which they are immersed. What we notice from these observations often becomes the basis for reflection. So as coaches, what do we often notice? Is it that things aren't going quite as you had planned? Is it that your athletes aren't performing in the way that you wanted? Is it that you don't seem to be getting the message across to your athletes that you hoped? Pinpointing problems and trying to work on ways in which these might be 'fixed' is central to much of the work that we do as coaches. It's even enshrined in Level 4 National Governing Body assessments of coaching. Here we see it in such assessment statements as, *"to recognise and correct negative performance."*

In general we are not that good at explaining what contributed to something being a great success or a total failure. We might feel a coaching session went 'ok', but when pressed to explain why, things can become more difficult. So it's important to move away from general feelings and opinions and focus on specific 'episodes' of success (or failure) and things in-between. So rather than ask you *why* you think you succeeded (or failed) at doing something, we want to invite you to write a short but vivid description of *what* you did in the past. To clarify, rather than asking, '*What* do you do?' or 'What do you *think* you do?'

Reflective activity:

Think about a specific instance where you where outstandingly good at doing something. Write half a page where you recall what you did, what you said, how, and what kinds of impact this had on those around you. If this feels like a lot of questions, you're right, it is! We are asking them because if we don't, there is a danger that you will simply write a description of what happened. Descriptions can be useful but they are not very helpful in pointing out to you what you need to do more of, less of, and so on, next time.

1. Write down the name of your specific coaching episode or practice encounter.

2. Then write half a page stating specifically what you did to be outstandingly good.

---

we are asking you to consider, 'What *did* you do?'

We suggest that you come back to your answer after about a week. At this point re-read what you have written. Try to look for BEHAVIOURS that led to this success. Ask yourself, *'How far can I/should I repeat these behaviours?'* Also, *'What can I control and what can't I?'* So therefore, *'What should I concentrate on?'* And don't worry about being modest. Just make sure that you can back up what you are saying with some kind of example or **evidence**! It's important to write about what you are good at and therefore what you want to do again and again. It's a myth to think that what's ONLY worth thinking and writing about are your problems. In other words the things you want to get rid of!

One thing that turns many people off when they are asked to reflect on something they have done (some action), is that they fail to see the value in doing this. They see it as a task without meaning. A task for someone else. Something that doesn't affect how they feel, what they think and might do in the future. In other words, it lacks purpose. To help you with this we need to ask you some more questions. They are *'does it matter'* type questions.

Reflective activity:

Again you need to be honest with yourself. So, in terms of doing reflection, please ask yourself:

1. How far does it matter *why* you are doing it?
2. How far does it matter *who* you are doing it with/to/for?
3. How far does it matter *when* you do it?
4. How far does it matter *what* it's about?

Resilience can be seen a strength, so it is worth reflecting upon. At work you may have noticed that some colleagues are simply less fazed by setbacks than others, clearly showing more resilience, whatever life throws at them, than others. People like this are able to learn from their experience, be adaptable and flexible according to the demands of their work/performance environment, are energised rather than drained by crises and problems, and other people actively choose to collaborate with them (Clarke and Nicholson, 2010). Some people are more resilient than others, but why?

Why do some people seem better able to bounce back from all manner of situations thrown at them, than others? We know that individuals respond differently to different events. So what's the key? Some people seem more able to exploit the positive events in their life. Some are proactive problem-solvers. Some have a tendency to tackle issues rather than avoid them. Some people seem to have a radar system that provides them with information of the need to change. Some seem able to keep things in perspective and see beyond the immediate pressures of their everyday working life. And crucially some know where to look for assistance. Arguably these are some of the characteristics of resilient people and even more evident is that these could potentially distinguish between those people who are great coaches and those who just coach. Reflection and strengths-based practices can play an important role in building resilience. One way to think about resilience is to think of it as the ability not to see failure, or failing, as something to dwell on, but as an opportunity to learn from and to move forward, excepting that failure is a part of life. If this sounds a bit negative, here is another view.

We suggest that resilience is based on two things;

(a) A belief in and commitment to what you're doing,

(b) Confidence that you can make things better.

There are at least four implications of taking this view. We suggest they are;

1. Being comfortable with who you are,

2. Being clear about your values,

3. Having other interests which provides a source of relief, even escape, and that help you get a sense of perspective on things,

4. Having drive and determination, matched with realistic optimism. In life and work we can't win all the battles!

A further view of resilience as a strength is that it is about keeping going in stressful situations, about bouncing back and not allowing yourself to be bogged down.

Positivity, strengths and job satisfaction

Positivity, as a strength, is also linked with job satisfaction. When people use their strengths in their job, most of the time, it is not surprising that they feel more positive about work. They get more pleasure from it and find it more meaningful. So two key reflective questions become, 'What % of last week did you spend doing things that you really like to do?' Or 'What % of last week did you spend playing to your strengths?' Answering these two questions mean that you have been able to identify how, and where, particular strengths, that you feel you have, can be used in your current role. If you draw a blank over this you may wish to reflect upon these questions. 'How far are there missed opportunities in your current role, where you could, in different circumstances, spend more time using particular strengths?' Or 'What new situations can you put yourself in, at work, to use particular strengths that you possess? Or finally, 'How could you expand your current role to make better use of particular strengths?'

Buckingham (2007) talks a lot about job satisfaction. He suggests that it is linked with the twin strategy of playing to your strengths *and* cutting out your weaknesses. If you can't cut them out, can't fix them, then perhaps, with practise, you might be able to contain them. The worst thing is hearing yourself say, 'I wish I would never have to do this type of activity again.' "*While it may feel like your entire job is contaminated, that's probably not true. In reality, just a few activities are ruining your days, corrupting everything else in your job. By identifying, naming and tagging them, (that is problems or weaknesses) you restore them to their actual size: little puffs of annoyance, not a radioactive haze*" (Buckingham, 2007, p 156).

As coaches you should feel inspired to engage in a continuous, creative and appreciative processes of reflection if you wish your practice to improve. Reflection can be triggered by many things, one of which is a question. This is why we are asking you so many! Questions are a good way to start the reflective process, particularly if you don't know what to reflect on. Others of you may wish to focus on your passions, proficiencies and priorities to instigate the process. You choose. As you progress through the book you might find yourself developing new ways to think reflectively within the coaching contexts that you work.

One final point is that we are hoping you are getting a clear message that this book provides a new and different view on coach/practice development and improvement. It is a view that emphasises using the power and potency of reflection to help coaches identify, develop and amplify what they *can* do, not just what they can't. This book therefore encourages you to look at your strengths and not always focus our attention to the problems in your practice and that of your athlete's performance. This might be one way in which we can generate more positive feelings that energise us into positive action. Throughout the book we advocate the use of a process we call *strengths-based reflective learning* and describe strategies to enable you to be the best that you can be. We argue that this is central to our professional development.

A summary:

1. Adaptations and modifications to your coaching practice may take the form of behaviour changes (doing something differently) and/or changes in attitude (feeling and thinking differently).

2. To sustain and develop your own performance, ask yourself these key reflective questions based on your coaching practice over the last 6-12 months: What have I learnt? What am I ready to leave behind? What's beginning to emerge? What's most important to me?

3. Collecting evidence can be a powerful tool in your development as a coach. This may involve gathering quantitative (e.g., match analysis data) and qualitative (e.g., discussions with a mentor or colleague). Ideally you will reflect on evidence from different sources, achieving method triangulation.

4. Reflect on how you can use these forms of evidence to understand the impact of your coaching on the performance of yourself, your athletes, and colleagues.

5. You can achieve happiness, well-being and optimal functioning as a coach through the twin processes of: (a) building positivity (b) identifying, using and developing new character and performance strengths.

6. Fundamental to a positive approach to coaching practice is identifying and developing your standout strengths; those skills and competencies you personally do best.

7. Reflection and strengths-based practices can play an important role in building resilience; the ability not to see failure as something to dwell on, but as an opportunity to learn and move forward.

8. Questions are a good way to start the reflective process. These may be asked by yourself or a trusted colleague. You may also wish to focus on your passions, proficiencies and priorities to instigate the process.

9. Strengths-based reflective practices encourage coaches to focus on what they **can do**, not just what they can't. By adopting this approach you can optimise and play to your strengths whilst reducing, effectively managing or containing your weaknesses.

PART 2

COACHING CAMEOS – POSITIVE REFLECTION and ACTION

This part of the book provides examples of 5 high performance coaches-in-action, highlighting their stand-out strengths. A key focus here is to reflect on how the coaches' different qualities, attributes, their coaching styles, strategies and characteristics, enable them to be successful in their particular performance environments. It is an illustration of the things we have been discussing in the Introduction and Part 1 of the book.

This part is also an illustration of one of the central principles of applied positive psychology namely, if you want to be successful, study success. Don't study failure and say, 'Oh lets learn from this. These mistakes and failures are things we should avoid!' If as a coach, you spend a lot of time studying under-achievement, failure and problems, all you learn is more about those things. Studying them will tell you very little about success, achievement and fulfilment.

COACHING CAMEO 1

Sir Clive Woodward

Theme: Reflection-for-action rather than having a game plan

Having played rugby union in the amateur era and graduated with a sports science degree and a PGCE, Sir Clive Woodward went on to represent England and the British Lions. He later worked for a multi-national corporation called

Xerox in Australia, where he also played for Manly and studied Southern Hemisphere rugby. Upon returning to England, Sir Clive started up his own equipment leasing company, gaining an understanding of business principles which he later applied to elite sports performance. Following successful periods as coach of Henley and London Irish, Sir Clive was appointed as the England National team's first professional coach in 1997. Sir Clive went on to lead England to the 2003 Grand Slam and victory in the IRB World Cup later that year.

In Lee et al.'s (2009) article, Sir Clive Woodward provides a detailed account of his coaching philosophy including his influences from business, strengths-based approaches to management and the celebrated notion of the 'critical non-essentials'. The main focus in this part of the book is on how Sir Clive developed a culture of learning and reflection amongst his players. This commences in the earliest stages of taking on a new team, when he believed it was vital to sit down with each player and encourage them to understand the team's strategic direction. Here Sir Clive illustrates how he achieves this initial 'buy in' from the players;

"I think allocating time to sit down and analyse a video of a game in order to understand why things happened... You need to ask the right questions and challenge the players to think about the decisions they make... This will allow your real style to come across after which, one-on-one sessions with players facilitate the development of operational standards. At league level you have so many players to organise, but you have to get the same message across to all of them."

Fostering this culture of reflection underlines the importance of having players who understand what they're doing on the pitch rather than expecting to simply carry out tasks in a 'machine-like' fashion. Sir Clive explains:

"The best debrief sessions should be led by the players. You want players in the room, knowing that they've done their homework. I would let them talk and then join the discussion if needed, simply to facilitate the analysis. Too often, coaches assume that they need to be the ones doing the talking and players simply sit down without actually engaging to any great extent... The more work you put in, the more clarity should come through and by encouraging players to take ownership, they will eventually understand and learn more."

The notion of having players learn and understand the game in depth is clearly central to Sir Clive's winning mentality. This is emphasised further as he believed players should even be able to teach technical skills themselves, if they are to maximise their development;

"With regard to skill development, the only way you can actually know if you have taught someone properly is whether they can teach you back... The big questions for me are 'is the athlete really learning the sport?'; 'are you engaging with them?'; 'could they do a degree in this sport?' If an athlete is serious about winning and performing, their technical knowledge has got to be as good as yours. In my opinion, the culture in many sports is that coaches are delivering knowledge to their players, but the players don't necessarily understand the need for this: they still maintain the mindset of 'when can we go out and train?' And 'why are we sitting here listening to all this?'"

Potentially uncomfortable for some practitioners, Sir Clive insists that on a technical level at least, athletes should be as knowledgeable as the coach. Promoting this level of engagement and self-awareness amongst players is key to developing a reflective team culture. This extends to players reflecting-in-action and thinking on their feet within games, making decisions according to the rapidly changing environment. Indeed, former England captain Martin Johnson revealed that Sir Clive never used the word 'game-plan', preferring instead to empower players to go out onto the field and play it how they see it. But whilst encouraging players to think for themselves on the pitch, preparing for high for performance (reflection-for-action) is also imperative;

"I feel that you can achieve so much training in the classroom, so when things do happen on the pitch, the players haven't just got a plan, but they're actually thinking 'What is the situation? We've got to win this game, but we've got to make the right decision.' You need to coach 'what if' scenarios... The concept of a 'game-plan' to me is very regimented. This philosophy is about encouraging players to think rather than just do! You cannot do enough thinking in advance of a situation."

Indeed, it was this emphasis on what Sir Clive terms 'pre-thinking' that led England to be the best prepared team in world rugby in 2003.

COACHING CAMEO 2

Andy Banks

Taking talent to its ceiling

Andy Banks is best known for being the coach of London 2012 bronze medallist diver Tom Daley. Under Banks' tutelage, Daley became World Champion on the 10 metre platform in 2009, and at the time of going to press, holds European and Commonwealth titles. Banks also guided Team GB Olympic synchro pair Tonia Couch and Sarah Barrow to a gold medal at the

2012 European Championships. He has held a range of international coaching roles since 1991, including that of Head Coach to the 2002 Commonwealth Games Team, the most successful England Team ever. Prior to his coaching career, Banks competed to national level himself before studying a degree in human movement. Now with over 30 years' experience as a diving coach, Banks is currently Head Coach and Director of Plymouth City Sport.

As detailed at length in Dixon et al.'s (2012) article, competing at only a modest level initially fuelled Andy Banks' ambition to develop the talent of others. Banks gained a deeper understanding of diving through studying biomechanics, physiology and psychology; something he now accredits to giving him the knowledge base needed to manage a multi-disciplinary environment. To this end, Banks believes the coach should lead the athlete development process with a 'jack of all trades' understanding, whilst using the analogy of a racing car to highlight the multiple dimensions and inputs into athletic performance.

Another metaphor used by Banks represents how the coach works with and builds on an athlete's existing talent;

"If you have quality clay then you can make a Ming Vase. If you don't then you might as well just stick with a load of coffee cups. Having said that you still need the skill to be able to mould it; you can't make a Ming Vase if you don't know what you're doing. So the two come together I think."

Here Banks illustrates how innate ability and the right coaching can help athletes fulfil their potential. This forms Banks' coaching philosophy and how he defines achievement as a coach;

"I'm a big believer that you do have to have talent to succeed but also if the coaching isn't correct then you're likely to limit the ceiling of what that talent can achieve. So my goal was to find the talent and then help it to achieve its ceiling... [achievement] is very much taking whatever kid it is to their ceiling. In terms of actually coaching [Daley] it's been relatively easy. Technique and mechanics are very interlinked, so learning how it works mechanically so you have a full understanding of exactly what it is you are trying to achieve I think is massively important. You can then mould what you see."

When it comes to 'moulding' athletes within a sport such as diving, coaches may do this over a relatively long period of time. For example, Banks has worked with Daley since the diver was nine years old. At the time of the London 2012 Games their coach-athlete relationship spanned almost ten years. Here, Banks outlines how he maintains a healthy, dynamic learning environment over such a long period;

"...you start off as a dictator and the kids down here somewhere because they haven't got a clue about anything so you tell them what to do. Then gradually that should change and you come up to more of a par and ultimately become the advisor...You know Tom [Daley] used to stand there and look around and gaze at people diving in and this and that. Now he's got a planned pre-prepared process for what he's going to do throughout the whole competition and he's completely in charge of that. I'm just a part of that at some point during the process. Then he comes up and we just talk about a couple of things to think about."

This evolving coach-athlete relationship is also evident in what Banks surprisingly labels as his greatest achievement to date. His self-proclaimed greatest success was helping a novice diver win a single Junior International tracksuit, stressing that she was never talented enough to perform at that level but through the efforts of the coach-athlete team, she reached and maybe even exceeded her ceiling. Whether it is Olympic medallists or divers competing at a local level, Andy Banks has helped athletes to reach their potential through an evolving pedagogical relationship and practical understanding of the multi-disciplinary nature of high performance sport.

COACHING CAMEO 3

Pia Sundhage

Portray positivity and convey confidence

One of the most respected coaches in women's football and widely regarded as one of the world's all-time greatest female players, Pia Sundhage was the first foreign coach and only the second woman to take charge of the United States Women's national team. While at the helm of the USA, Sundhage won Gold medals at both the 2008 and 2012 Olympics, in addition to winning the coveted Algarve Cup in 2008. In September 2012, Sundhage stepped down from her role with the USA, aiming to replicate her achievements with the National team of her native Sweden.

Despite the USA maintaining its world number one ranking throughout Pia Sundhage's reign, her journey was far from plain sailing. Sundhage took over at a time when the USA's domestic league competition had become defunct, undoubtedly impacting on the quality of the national team. More importantly, the team had recently exited the 2007 World Cup after a humiliating 4–0 semi-final defeat at the hands of Brazil, the biggest loss in the team's history. This was followed by public in-fighting amongst players and the acrimonious departure of her predecessor.

Charged with the responsibility of restoring broken morale and damaged reputations, Sundhage's response was far from conventional; she regaled the team, guitar in hand, singing Bob Dylan's "The Times They Are a Changin'." With a touch of eccentricity, Sundhage was already known in Sweden for her free spirit and tendency to break into song, and her choice of track was very fitting. Entering a difficult, argumentative environment may have led some coaches to forcibly exert their authority but this display of warmth and composure became a trademark of Sundhage's success. Indeed, she claims; "It's absolutely vital that even if you're feeling stressed, your players should absolutely never see it. In fact, as often as possible they should see the opposite" (Woitalla, 2012).

Having stabilised a fractured team, Sundhage began to change the way the Americans played, making them more reliant on possession and technical skill than on mere athleticism, speed and fitness. Furthermore, she coached with a calm presence, facilitating the belief that victory was always possible, even when it seemed frustratingly remote. This was particularly evident in the World Cup qualifying tournament in October 2010. The USA had lost to Mexico in the semi-finals and therefore needed to win a playoff against Italy to go through; the USA had never failed to qualify for the Women's World Cup. Even under this intense pressure, when asked about the way her team would have to qualify, Sundhage said;

"OK, we need to take a different road to the World Cup and look at it in a positive way. The glass is half full. It's been a bumpy road, but we need to enjoy it and it will take us all the way [to the World Cup]" (Foudy, 2012).

Not only did the USA qualify, but they made it to the final, where they were narrowly beaten on penalties by Japan.

Sundhage's players visibly benefitted from her relaxed, positive approach to coaching which midfielder Heather O'Reilly calls "glass half full to the max." Similarly, goalkeeper Hope Solo said "She's more laid-back than any coach I have ever had. She wanted to bring fun back to the game" (Longman, 2012). This style has also been acclaimed by one of Sundhage's predecessors, former World Cup winning coach Anson Dorrance; "she exudes a wonderful kind of optimism and positivity and has a tremendous calm manner that I think is conveyed very effectively to her players" (Woitalla, 2012).

As a two time Olympic gold medal winning coach, Sundhage's approach is not only personable but has helped her to deliver success at the highest level. Her composed style is not just a personality trait but a deliberate strategy to get results, as Sundhage revealed in an interview;

"I try to use my body language to emphasise what is good. I'm really happy to hear that when you watch the women's team play you think I'm calm, because that's what I want my players to believe, because I have faith in the way we play and in our players. I emphasise the good things. I'm looking for good things, instead of doing the opposite and try constantly to adjust mistakes" " (Woitalla, 2012).

With the extreme pressure and expectation of high performance sport well documented, Pia Sundhage's approach enabled her players to enjoy and express themselves in competitive situations. Sundhage's style has won titles and the respect of her athletes, as summed up by one of her former players, legendary forward Abby Wambach; "I love Pia so much because she has shown me what it's like to love the game" (Longman, 2012).

COACHING CAMEO 4

Dave Brailsford

The aggregation of marginal gains

Having competed as a professional cyclist in France, Dave Brailsford returned his native Britain to study a Degree in Sport Science and Psychology. He has been employed by British Cycling since 1996, ultimately reaching the position of performance director. Brailsford led the GB cycling team to victories at the Athens, Beijing and London Olympics as they became the greatest track cycling team in modern history. Arguably the most successful British Olympic coach of his era, Brailsford managed his Team GB role alongside that of Sky Team principal, through which he oversaw both Bradley Wiggins' 2012 Tour de France victory and Chris Froome's repeat of this success the following year.

Central to Dave Brailsford's approach to improving the performance curve is his meticulous, analytical coaching style. This is highlighted by his mantra of analysing each small element of professional cycling to see if anything could be done better. Every athlete and member of staff is encouraged to reflect on the tiniest things that could make a minute difference to their performance. Such incremental improvements have included; alcohol sprayed on tyres to reduce friction at the start; special mattresses to help athletes get sufficient sleep, lessons in hand washing to ward off illness, and electrically heated hot pants which athletes wear between races to keep muscles at optimal temperature.

In isolation these factors may not make a significant difference but the accumulation of these improvements could shave crucial milliseconds off race time, ultimately gaining the edge over competitors. Brailsford calls this 'the aggregation of marginal gains', an approach which he believes can be applied to other aspects of life;

"Take cycling out of it for a minute... we thought about personal excellence, how to get the person to be the best that they can be, and then we applied it to cycling. I think the model we've come up with and the way we work can be applied to anything really. The best lawyer, the best dentist, the best anything, so I think there's a philosophy there that's quite interesting".

Whilst technical improvements are strongly emphasised, also central to the marginal gains strategy is Brailsford's ability to put logic ahead of emotion. For example, he brought in a psychiatrist, who has asked the team members to 'park their chimp'; a term used to encourage staff and athletes to remove their emotional and irrational thoughts from the sporting arena and focus solely on the process of achieving excellence.

This culture of logical, analytical thinking is reflected by Dave Brailsford's personality and demeanour which appears highly focused and pensive yet has an edge of authority. Indeed, childhood friend and former Welsh international footballer Malcolm Allen describes a young Brailsford as "quiet" yet demonstrating "strength of character, mental strength and an attitude to win."

These attributes are clearly beneficial when working in the intensity of track and road cycling, however Brailsford's relentless pursuit of sporting excellence can sometimes be difficult to work with. Here, two time gold medallist Geraint Thomas elaborates; "Sometimes people struggle with that [management style]... He's full-on and committed and expects everyone else around him to do that, and if you don't its 'sorry but you've got to go' so he's pretty ruthless." This ruthless streak holds no prisoners as Brailsford is even reported to have threatened cycling legend Bradley Wiggins with the sack after a below par performance at the 2010 Tour de France.

The GB performance director has always maintained that his team demands intensity above the norm, potentially making it an uncomfortable place to be.

"You've got times when you need to push people hard, to push people out of the comfort zone. I know from different personal experiences that unless I'm frightened or scared or something, really concerned about something ... If I am, then I work really, really hard."

Whilst this performance environment can be intense and difficult, it may help to form the resilience and hard edge that athletes need at the highest levels of cycling performance. This approach has delivered success beyond expectations, and Brailsford's ambition is unlikely to stop here as he outlines his plans for Rio 2016; "We won seven golds from 10 events in Beijing. We've won seven golds from 10 events [in London]. So of course it's possible to win all 10."

Finally, in addition to his extraordinary attention to detail, analytical skills and ruthless streak, perhaps a more understated quality of Brailsford's is his sense of humour. Such was the extent of Team GB's dominance at London 2012, their arch rivals in the French camp questioned the legitimacy of their wheel design, to which Brailsford replied "the trick with our wheels is that they're round, really round".

COACHING CAMEO 5

Wayne Smith

To learn from the past but not live in the past

Former New Zealand international rugby player Wayne Smith began coaching Super 12 team Crusaders in 1997, subsequently winning two titles before being appointed All Blacks coach in 1999. In 2001 Smith became head coach at Northampton Saints where he led the club to the Powergen cup final and Heineken cup qualification, before returning to the All Blacks in 2004. As assistant to Sir Graham Henry, Smith coached the National team for seven years, culminating in the ultimate accolade as the All Blacks won the IRB World Cup in 2011. Despite an offer to return to International Rugby with England, Smith opted to stay in New Zealand with the Chiefs, who he recently guided to their first Super League title.

This cameo primarily draws on an interview featured in Kidman's (2005) book on athlete-centred coaching, which is central to Wayne Smith's coaching philosophy. Specifically, Smith adopts the Game Sense method to coaching which involves training using modified games to replicate the playing environment whilst developing decision making skills and intuitive play. Questioning and discussion are also fundamental to this approach, giving athletes more power and ownership of their performance. For instance, Smith incorporates group reflection using video and statistical analysis, empowering his players through a strengths-based approach; "we do check points every month to ensure they are getting on-going improvements and are working on making their strengths stronger." Through positivity, Smith creates an environment which allows players to make mistakes as part of their learning process, insisting the coach's job is to "make sure they're not making the same mistakes over and over."

Such an approach to high performance was alien in Smith's playing career and he asserts that whilst learning from his previous coaches was valuable, it only formed part of his education as a coach;

"I read a lot of corporate-type coaching and business management books. Complementing our traditional values, rugby's heritage, with a vision-driven process and systems-based model has stood me in good stead. I like to learn from the past but not live in the past."

This illustrates Smith's innovative nature and openness to a variety of knowledge sources which have helped mould his philosophy and practice, something he strongly recommends to the coaching fraternity; "I think coaches need to look at things on merit and understand that just because they've played the game, they don't know everything about it."

Whilst internationally recognised as a top class coach now, Smith's innovative approach to high performance coaching was not well received initially; "One of the problems I faced early on in my career was that people thought I was a tree hugger, too soft. There was a public perception that I wasn't tough enough." Rather than cave in to this pressure and revert to traditional methods, Smith demonstrated resilience and belief in his values to ultimately achieve success. Indeed, facing adversity and coming out of it stronger is core to Smith's character;

"The coach has to be resilient and consistently optimistic under pressure. After five games in the 1998 Super 12, we [Canterbury Crusaders] were last and coming in for a lot of criticism. One of my sons (Joshua) was in hospital for some major surgery and my contract was up at the end of the season. In this situation, you have to lead the way; the players deserve your best effort every day. It takes huge reserves of energy to dig deep and keep fighting, but once you give up, the players will give up. Your job is to keep hope alive for yourself and your players."

Here Smith shows how a coach's resilience and positivity can resonate with their athletes to accomplish long term success despite difficult circumstances. Through openness to learning and resilience to the pressures of convention,

Wayne Smith has used innovative methods to achieve remarkable success, building positive environments for high performance.

PART 3

SOME USEFUL THEORETICAL PERSPECTIVES

Currently **the self** as a focus for continuous improvement, remains at the forefront of much psychological research. One outcome of this has been the generation of theoretical perspectives (or you could call them, frameworks) pertaining to the self in the context of psysical activity and sport. In the title of this book we use the two words **improving performance.** At this part of the book we wish to introduce you to two specific terms within this. The first might be called, (a) **SKILL-enhancement** which is about your performance, or what you can do. This includes your real and perceived competence and ability. The other can be called, (b) **SELF-enhancement** which is about the use of your character qualities and personality traits that support, or constrain (a) .... your performance. But as we have tried to make clear, the coach is not a free 'agent'. There are many contextual things (socio-cultural and politico-economic) that inhibit or liberate performance. However having said that, this book makes a contribution to literature in an era where greater attention and development is being placed on the self as an **'agent of change'.** This is sports coaches, managers, sports therapists etc. who can generate and positively use evidence to influence and improve their own and other's performance.

So where does theory come in? Its easy to be put off by this word. It can sound very abstract. When we use it, we can get into challenging territory. One thing to appreciate about theory is that there are many of them. A second thing is that they (theories) are like 'lenses' through which to look at complicated and changing phenomena that we find in sport. Many theories help us make sense of the complexities of practice and some can help explain things. Some even help us appreciate what might, or might not, be usefully 'controlled' in some way. Other theories help us predict what might happen if we do this or that, in certain conditions.

Some people feel there is a 'gap' between theory and practice. One consequence of this is that those in coach education and those studying on various award-bearing programmes, often have to think about the *application* of theoretical knowledge to practice stituations. If we do this we have to be very careful we don't fall into the trap of force-fitting our coaching realities into some already pre-formed theoretical framework. This achieves nothing positive, only potential frustration! It might be useful to think of theory and practice as two complementary kinds of knowledge, interacting with each other, with one informing and transforming the other. Theoretical knowledge, just like all other kinds of knowledge, is *'contested'*. This means that not everyone will agree with it, value it and believe in it.

In this part of the book we have identified 5 theoretical perspectives which underpin much of the applied content in this book.

PERSPECTIVE 1

THE BROADEN and BUILD THEORY

This is one of the most important theories to emerge from the new field of positive psychology. It is very relevant to sport performance and coach education. It was developed by Professor Barbara Fredrickson from the USA. Fredrickson's (1998, 2001, 2003, 2004) *broaden-and-build theory links* how you feel with what you can do. In her work she promotes the notion of *'positivity'*. Her theory describes and explains the impact a number of positive emotions, (e.g. a sense of achievement, joy, interest, pride and love), have on the things we do and how well we do them.

A key proposition is that these positive emotions **broaden** an individual's momentary thought-action repertoire. This means when we feel positive, we are generally more open-minded, more receptive to new ideas, more adaptive and more flexible (Fredrickson & Branigan, 2005). For example the joy of engaging in physical activity sparks the urge to play, interest in a (new) sport sparks the urge to explore, contentment that comes from a hard fought victory sparks the urge to savour.

The broadened mindset arising from these positive emotions is contrasted to the narrowed mindsets sparked by many negative emotions and their associated action tendencies, such as to attack or flee. In other words when we feel more negative we feel much less prepared, and able, to consider alternatives, to 'play' with new ideas and ways of doing things and to consider options.

A second key proposition of this theory is that positive emotions *build* an individual's personal resources and ability to be resilient to buffer against future emotional setbacks. These can range from physical (better energy management) and intellectual resources (learning new things), to social (build positive relationships) and psychological ones (build a sense of identity and goal orientation). Importantly, these resources function as reserves that can be drawn on later to improve the prospect of performing well under pressure, successful coping, and well-being.

Fredrickson (2009) argues that we can actually work at increasing our sense of positivity (which is linked with self-regard) and that this can:
· Make us feel good
· Change how our mind normally works
· Transform how we normally do things
· Put the brakes on negativity

Fredrickson and Losada (2005) and Fredrickson (2006) took the broaden-and-build theory a step further, by proposing that an individual's degree of flourishing and well-being could be predicted by that person's ratio of positive to negative emotions over time, which they termed the "positivity ratio."

PERSPECTIVE 2

SELF-DETERMINATION THEORY (SDT)

This is connected with motivation. Any coach wishing to get the best out of the athletes they work with should be concerned with understanding how to motivate them. The importance of understanding individual participation motives and the factors affecting individual motivation so that a coach can assist an athlete to find energy, mobilize effort and persist at tasks, is paramount in the sports environment. Self-Determination Theory, (Ryan & Deci, 2000) represents a broad framework for the study of human motivation and personality. This work is based on the premise that humans have 3 innate needs:

- To be in relationships with others
- To experience competence
- To function with autonomy

Conditions supporting individual experiences of relatedness, competence, and autonomy, support or limit our motivation and therefore our engagement in activities.

Coaches need to be concerned with motivation — how to move themselves or others to act. Some are motivated by external factors such as reward systems, grades, evaluations, or the opinions they fear others might have of them. Yet just as frequently, others are motivated from within, by personal interests, curiosity and the will to win. The interplay between the extrinsic forces acting on us and the intrinsic motives and needs inherent within us is the territory of Self-Determination Theory (SDT).

When we look at the world of sport and exercise rewards are used extensively to enhance and reinforce motivation. Indeed, advocates of extrinsic rewards argue that rewards increase motivation, enhance learning and increase the desire to participate. However, while the systematic use of rewards can produce some desired behaviour changes, it is not always a given.

For example, providing individuals with rewards for their participation for an already interesting activity often leads to a decrease in intrinsic motivation due to a shift in perceived autonomy, or locus of causality (referring to actions initiated by external or internal force). By rewarding people, subsequent involvement in the task can be reduced when the reward is no longer available. This is explained by the over-justification effect, where with the use of expected rewards causes a shift in perceptions from intrinsic to extrinsic. The reward over-justifies the behaviour.

Research using this work has looked at how controlling versus autonomy-supportive environments impact on functioning and wellness, as well as performance and persistence. Furthermore, creating environments where relatedness and competence can be enhanced have been seen to foster engagement during specific tasks. This body of applied research has led to considerable specification of techniques, including goal structures and ways of communicating that have proven effective at promoting and maintaining motivation (Ryan & Deci, 2000).

PERSPECTIVE 3

ATTRIBUTION THEORY

Involvement in sport, by its very nature, exposes individuals to an environment where their performances are instantly judged and evaluated, both by themselves and others around them. As a result, the impetus to explain the outcomes that have prevailed becomes heightened as we attempt to attribute causes to these events that occurred around us. This process is illustrated in

Attribution theory, popularised by Weiner (1985, 1986, 1991), Weiner et al (1971) and Rees, et al (2005).

Weiner (1985) developed a theoretical framework founded on the premise that people try to determine why people do what they do by interpreting causes to an event or behaviour. In sport we might see this when a coach asks the question "why did we suffer that defeat today?" or "what led to our victory?" The work holds that there are literally thousands of possible explanations for success and failure, but the most important factors affecting attributions about achievement are ability, effort, task difficulty and luck. These attributions can be classified along 3 causal dimensions:

- Locus of control (internal vs. external)
- Stability (do causes change over time or not)
- Controllability (causes that one can control e.g., skill, vs. causes that one can't e.g., the actions of others).

Weiner (1986) predicted that stable attributes will lead to a greater degree of certainty regarding future outcomes than will unstable, thus will lead to an increased certainty regarding future outcomes. Unstable attributions will lead to reduced certainty about the future or the expectation that the future will be different from the past. It is this that will have influence over factors such as how much motivation we demonstrate for subsequent performances. For example, if you expect the outcome to occur again in the future, it is more likely an individual will to be motivated and confident. If they don't' expect it to occur regularly, motivation and confidence will not be enhanced.

In 1993, Biddle provided an account of the attribution process that takes place, identifying the mechanisms through which individuals can be impacted by the attributions made. This is depicted in Figure 3 below.

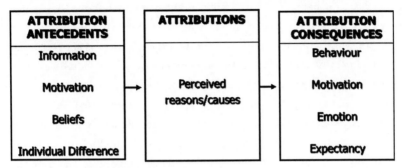

Figure 3. Biddle's (1993) attribution process

In attempts to develop our understanding of this area further, Buchanan & Seligman (1995) looked at optimism vs. pessimism in their work on explanatory style. A pessimistic explanatory style would be identified in an individual blaming themselves for a loss and feeling powerless to change, so the losing streak will continue. This often results in a loss of motivation. Conversely, an optimistic explanatory style sees athletes more open to learning from defeat and committing to working harder in the future. As a result individuals can develop a healthy resilience and keep confidence levels in tack and positive outlooks about their future performances.

PERSPECTIVE 4

ATTACHMENT THEORY

It goes without saying that a key determinant of coaching effectiveness and sporting success is based on the quality of the relationship that is formed between coach and athlete. Indeed, if we want to be able to get the best out of those that we work with, the nature of the relationship that is formed, built and developed is critical to creating an environment where individuals *want* to work for each other to achieve their individual and shared goals. With that in mind, Attachment theory (Bowlby, 1969, 1982) has been used extensively within social psychology to examine factors, such as relationship quality, but has only more recently began to receive the same attention within the context of sports research. This transfer into sport is unsurprising given the inherent interpersonal aspects of sports participation.

Attachment theory (Bowlby, 1969, 1982) offers an established framework aimed at understanding the bonds that are formed in close relationships. Bowlby's (1969, 1982) initial work was based upon observations of how infants interacted with their primary caregiver, usually their mother. Ainsworth, Blehar, Waters and Wall (1978) furthered the research in this area by presenting a categorisation of attachment into 3 attachment styles:

- Secure – evident in individuals who display confidence in the availability of their close other to provide them with comfort and support in times of need. They also display reduced distress upon proximity to the caregiver following separation (Felton & Jowett, 2013).

- Anxious-ambivalent (insecure attachment style) – displayed in individuals who have a strong desire for proximity and intimacy with their caregiver despite the conditions (distressing or non-distressing). These individuals become angry and upset with the caregiver following separation (Felton & Jowett, 2013).

- Avoidant (insecure attachment style) – displayed in individuals who exhibit little distress during separation from their close other and also display few attempts at maintaining or sustaining contact (Felton & Jowett, 2013).

So what does this mean to those of us working in sport, and specifically sports coaching? Fundamentally, research has established that those individuals who are securely attached to close others report greater well-being than those insecurely attached. This highlights the links between secure attachment style and optimal functioning (for review see Mikulincer & Shaver, 2007). In sport, the amount of satisfaction derived from participation could be impacted by coach-athlete relations and the athlete's attachment style relative to their coach. Davis and Jowett (2014) investigated coach-athlete relationship satisfaction and sport satisfaction to determine if they were associated with attachment style. Findings indicated that insecure attachment (anxious and avoidant) to the coach resulted in perceptions of reduced relationship and sport satisfaction.

PERSPECTIVE 5

A THEORY-OF-ACTION

We are going to present this theory in more diagrammatic way. We hope this will help you appreciate how central and significant this theory is to improving your practice. If you use any search engine, you will find lots about this theory and its application.

You can look at a good explanation of this if you search for:

Argyris, C., & Schön, D. (1978) Organizational learning: A theory of action perspective, Reading, Mass: Addison Wesley.

In essence this theory helps us understand the importance of matching what we say (words) with what we do (actions). A good match is called a 'congruence'. But if we say one thing, then do something else, we are what is called a living contradiction. Sometimes a mis-match between what we say (our espoused theory) and what we do (our theory in action) is inevitable and especially in a fast changing, complex and often unpredictable performance context. So don't go and beat yourself up each time your actions don't follow your words. But if this happens repeatedly, it's certainly something to reflect upon.

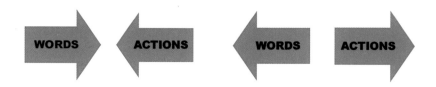

CONGRUENCE – match between what you say and do

CONSEQUENCES – un/intended for self, athletes, sports organization etc.

Within this theoretical perspective there is also the notion of *learning loops* (see Figure 4 below). Much coaching could be described as *single loop* learning. In other words the coach is focused on improving and practising skills and techniques (behaviours) and linking the successful acquisition of these to 'results'. So a key question for coaches when they are practising single loop learning is, 'are we doing things right?' **Double loop** learning is when the coach thinks deeply about the purpose/s and value/s behind what they are doing. It's when a coach is conscious of putting their values (beliefs) into action (behaviours) and how this then manifests itself in results. So the key question now becomes, 'Am I doing the right things?' **Triple loop** learning is where the coach widens their coaching lens and takes a very holistic view of what they are doing, how and why. This kind of learning loop usually, explicitly, takes into consideration broader organisational issues, historical, political and social ones.

Figure 4.   Single, Double and Triple Learning Loops (Argyris, C., & Schön, D. 1978)

Learning Loops

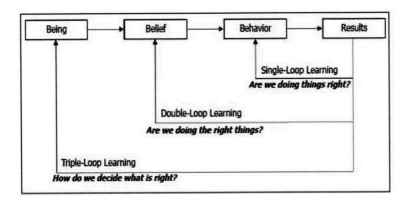

PART 4

Positively Coaching for Greatness

This book aimed to make a contribution to the process of being the best you can be, as a coach. Part of the bigger picture is the need to create a positive learning environment that supports coach education and continuous professional development. This can be called a **'positive reflective performance environment'** where coaches place themselves front and central in their own learning.

Typically when using reflective practices, coaches will step back after a training session, or sporting event, and evaluate what happened in order to know how best to proceed. As we have tried to show throughout this book, there is no 'one best way' to do this and to develop coaching expertise. However without systematic reflections-on-action, any kind of development will be stunted, in jeopardy or even deluded. It is not rocket science to appreciate that performance expectations on coaches can be intense (Olusoga et al, 2010). This can range, for example, from athletes under-performing in competition, pressures from 'The Board', from the media, from National Governing Bodies, from fans and conflicts between sporting personnel. Given this, we argue that coach development programmes have to positively address this and support coach education by keeping up with new disciplinary and pedagogical initiatives that serve to enable coaches to develop their 'edge' and to be the best they can be, everyday. This requires the generation and positive use of 'evidence' of improvement (Faull & Cropley, 2009, Neil, et al, 2013).

There are many things that constantly compete for a coach's attention. Three more obvious ones are the need for: (a) **Achievement** - attention given to goal attainment, results and performance. (b) **Innovation** – attention that needs to be given to doing the same things differently and doing different things.

(c) **Well-being** – how their own and their athlete's physical, mental, emotional, social and spiritual needs and wants are being addressed. These multiple and often competing areas can create tensions that the coach needs to try to successfully manage. Prioritisation is essential. This can only be achieved when coaches reflect on their practices, their athlete's well-being and the demands of performance environment within which both are embedded. As we have tried to explain and illustrate in this book, coach education programmes are strengthened if they enable coaches to ask themselves **'reflective questions'** and then offer appropriate support to enable the coach to do something with their responses. We suggest that it's vital to balance deficit-type questions (what went wrong, who was responsible and why?) with strength-based ones (what was successful and positive, why and how can this be amplified?). Six standard reflective questions (in addition to those we explained earlier) are:

1) *What am I doing?* (awareness)
2) *How successful am I?* (appreciating)
3) *What is an even better way of doing this?* (imagine)
4) *What do I need to do to achieve this?* (design)
5) *Is this what I should be doing* (judgement)
6) *How far am I being the best I can be, everyday?* (evaluation)

We suggest that for coaches to be the best example of themselves, everyday, it's important for them to appreciate that reflection and its practices, are not a frivolous, luxury and time consuming process. Learning through systematic, rigorous and critical reflection on their practices, especially if done together, is a necessity if they are to constantly improve and be responsive to changing sports performance circumstances. In this way, *self-reflection* transforms into *self-realisation* and coaching to your full potential.

We would argue that everything in this book is relevant to how you coach and more importantly, how you *choose* to coach. In other words what you learn through positive reflections on your practice, should help govern how and why you make the coaching choices you do. In Figure 4 below we have tried to summarise much of the essence of this book. We are going to be bold and suggest that if you can put the following 4 key **capabilities into action**, you may create opportunities for yourself to *positively coach for greatness*.

Fig. 4   Positively Coaching for Greatness

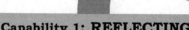

Capability 1: REFLECTING

Positively on your strengths and growth points

Remembering — What works & why as well as what needs attention.

Capability 2: ACCEPTING

Responsibility to continuously learn and develop

Owning — Your professional/coaching development agenda.

Capability 3: POSITIVE ACTION

To always try to be the best you can be

Being consistent — Matching what you say with what you do.

Capability 4: BEING AUTHENTIC

Being true to your values & acting with integrity

Appreciating — How to put your character & performance strengths to work.

REFERENCES AND USEFUL READING

Ainsworth, M., Blehar, M., Waters, E., & Wall, S., (1978), Patterns of attachment: A psychological study of the strange situation. Hillsdale, N.J.: Erlbaum.

Argyris, C., & Schön, D., (1978), Organizational learning: A theory of action perspective, Reading, Mass: Addison Wesley.

Barnson, S., (2014), The Authentic Coaching Model: A Grounded Theory of Coaching, International Sports Coaching Journal, 1, 61 – 74.

BBC.(2012). Dave Brailsford.
http://www.bbc.co.uk/iplayer/episode/b011sqkq/Profile_Dave_Brailsford/
Accessed 04.09.2012.

Biddle, S., (1993), Attribution research and sport psychology. In R. N. Singer, M. Murphey, & L. K. Tennant (Eds.), Handbook of research on sport psychology (pp. 437–464). New York: Macmillan.

Bloom, G., Stevens, D., & Wickwire, T., (2003), Expert coaches' perceptions of team building. *Journal of Applied Sport Psychology, 15*(2), 129–143.

Bowlby J., (1969/1982), Attachment and Loss, volume 1, *Attachment*, Basic Books, New York.

Buckingam, M, (2011), Standout. Nashville, TN: Thomas Nelson.

Buckingham, M. & Coffman, C., (2005), First, break all the rules: What the world's greatest manager's do differently. Pocket Books, London.

Buckingham, M., (2007), Go put your strengs to work: Six powerful steps to achieve outstanding performance. Simon & Schuster UK Ltd, London.

Buckingham, M., & Clifton, D., (2001), Now, discover your strengths: How to develop your talents and those of the people you manage. London: Simon & Schuster.

Buchanan, G., & Seligman, M., (1995), Explanatory style. Hillsdale, NJ: Erlbaum.

Cassidy, T., Jones, R.L., & Potrac, P., (2009), Understanding sports coaching: The social, cultural and pedagogical foundations of coaching practice (2nd ed.). London: Routledge.

Chan, J. & Clifford, M., (2011), The Value of Emotional Intelligence for High Performance Coaching, International Journal of Sports Science & Coaching Volume 6 · Number 3, 315-328

Clark, D., (2006), Motivating to win: How to create, inspire and motivate a high performing team. Liskeard: Exposure Publishing.

Clarke, J. & Nicholson, J., (2010), Resilience: Bounce back from whatever life throws at you. Crimson Publishing: Richmond, Surrey.

Coe, S., (2009), The winning mind: My inside track on great leadership. London: Headline.

Collins, D. & Abraham, A., (2009), Identifying and Developing level Four-ness in Performance Coaches. sportscoach UK.

Côté, J. & Gilbert, W., (2009), An integrative definition of coaching effectiveness and expertise. International Journal of Sport Science and Coaching, 4, 307-232.

Cropley, B. Miles, A., & Peel, J., (2012), Reflective practice: Value of, issues, and developments, Sportscoach UK.

Cushion, C. Et al, (2006), Locating the coaching process in practice: models 'for' and 'of' coaching, Research Quarterly for Exercise and Sport, Volume 11, Issue 1, 388-99.

Cushion, C.J., (2007), Modelling the Complexity of the Coaching Process, International Journal of Sports Science and Coaching, 2, 4, 395-401.

Cushion, C., Armour, K. & Nelson, L., (2009), Coach Learning and Development: A Review of Literature. Leeds, sportscoach UK.

Davis, L & Jowett, S (2014), Coach-athlete attachment and the quality of the coach-athlete relationship: implications for athlete's well-being, Journal of Sports Sciences, 32(15), pp.1454-1464,

Dixon, M., Lee, S. & Ghaye, T. (2013), Reflective practices for better sports coaches and coach education: shifting from a pedagogy of scarcity to abundance in the run-up to Rio 2016, Reflective Practice: International and Multidisciplinary Perspectives, Vol. 14, No. 5, 585–599.

Dixon, M., Lee, S., & Ghaye, T. (2012), Coaching for Performance: an Interview with Olympic Diving Coach, Andy Banks. Reflective Practice: International and Multidisciplinary Perspectives, 13 (3), pp. 339-354.

Donaldson, S., Csikszentmihalyi, M. & Nakamura, J. (Eds) (2011), Applied Positive Psychology, Psychology press, Hove.

Faull, A., & Cropley, B., (2009), Reflective learning in sport: a case study of a senior level triathlete, Reflective Practice: International and Multidisciplinary Perspectives,10, pp325-339.

Felton, L and Jowett, S., (2013), The mediating role of social environmental factors in the associations between attachment styles and basic needs satisfaction, Journal of Sports Sciences, 31(6), pp.618-628.

Fletcher, D., & Wagstaff, C., (2009), Organizational psychology in elite sport: Its emergence, application and future. Psychology of Sport and Exercise, 10(4), 427–434.

Foudy, J. (2012), Pia's calm through the storms redefined U.S. team http://espn.go.com/espnw/news-commentary/article/8336924/espnw-pia-sundhage-calm-storms-redefined-us-women-soccer-team Accessed 27.11.2014.

Fredrickson, B., (1998), What good are positive emotions? Review of General Psychology, 2, 300-319.

Fredrickson, B., (2001), The role of positive emotions in positive psychology: The broaden-and-build theory of positive emotion. American Psychologist, 56, 218-226.

Fredrickson, B., (2003), The value of positive emotions. American Scientist, 91, 330- 335.

Fredrickson, B., (2004), The broaden-and-build theory of positive emotions. *Philosophical transactions of the Royal society of London Series B – biological sciences, 359,* (1449), 1367 – 1377.

Fredrickson, B., & Joiner, T. (2002), Positive emotions trigger upward spirals toward emotional well-being, Psychological Science, Vol. 13, No. 2, p. 172-175.

Fredrickson, B., & Branigan, C., (2005), Positive emotions broaden the scope of attention and thought-action repertoires. Cognition and Emotion, 19, 313-332.

Fredrickson B., & Losada M., (2005), "Positive affect and the complex dynamics of human flourishing." *American Psychologist,* 60 (7): 678–86.

Fredrickson, B., (2006), Unpacking positive emotions: Investigating the seeds of human flourishing. *Journal of Positive Psychology, 1,* 57–60.

Fredrickson, B., (2009), Positivity: Groundbreaking research reveals how to embrace the hidden strength of positive emotions, overcome negativity, and thrive. New York: Crown Publications.

Ghaye, T. (2011), Teaching and Learning through Reflective Practice: A practical guide for positive action, Routledge, Oxon.

Ghaye, T., Lee, S. Shaw, D. & Chesterfield, G. (2009), When winning is not enough: learning through reflections on the 'best-self', Reflective Practice: International and Multidisciplinary Perspectives, 10:3, 385 – 401.

Gilbert, W. & Trudel, P., (2004), The role of the coach: How model youth team sport coaches frame their roles. *The Sport Psychologist, 18,* 21–43.

Gilbert, W. D. & Trudel, P. (2005), Learning to coach through experience: Conditions that influence reflection. *The Physical Educator, 62,* 32-43.

Gogarty, P. & Williamson, I., (2009), Winning at all odds: Sporting gods and their demons, p. 221.

Grout, J., & Perrin, S. (2004), Mind games: Inspirational lessons from the world's biggest sports stars. Chichester: Capstone.

Hanin, Y. (Ed.) (2000), Emotions in sport. Champaign, IL: Human Kinetics.

Jones, R., (Ed.). (2005), The sports coach as educator: Reconceptualising sports coaching. London: Routledge.

Jones, R. (2007), Coaching redefined: an everyday pedagogical endeavour. *Sport Education and Society*, 12, 159-173.

Jones, R.L., & Wallace, M. (2005), Another bad day at the training ground: Coping with ambiguity in the coaching context. *Sport, Education and Society*, 10(1), 119-134.

Jones, R. & Wallace, M. (2006), The coach as 'orchestrator': More realistically managing the complex coaching context. In Jones, R. (Ed.) *The sports coach as educator: Reconceptualising sports coaching.* Abingdon, Routledge.

Kaiser, R., (2009), The perils of accentuating the positive. Hogan Press, OK.

Kidman, L., (2005), Athlete-Centred Coaching: Developing Inspired and Inspiring People. IPC Print Resources. Auckland, NZ.

Knowles, Z., & Gilbourne, D., (2004), Reflective practice for sports psychologists: Concepts, models, practical implications and thoughts on dissemination. The Sport Psychologist, 18, 188-203.

Knowles, Z., Borrie, A., & Telfer, H., (2005), Towards the reflective sports coach: Issues of context, education and application. Ergonomics, 48, 1711-1720.

Kyndt, T. & Rowell, S., (2012), Achieving Excellence in High Performance Sport, Bloomsbury, London.

Lee, S. Dixon, M. & Ghaye, T., (2014), Coaching for performance: Realising the Olympic Dream, Routledge, Oxon.

Lee, S., Dixon, M., Ghaye, T., & (with a contribution from Beth Tweddle, MBE), (2012), Realising the Olympic dream – bring on the alchemists. Reflective Practice: International and Multidisciplinary Perspectives, 13, 327-338.

Lee, S., Shaw, D., Chesterfield, G. & Woodward, C., (2009), Reflections from a World Champion: an interview with Sir Clive Woodward, Director of Olympic

Performance, the British Olympic Association, Reflective Practice: International and Multidisciplinary Perspectives, 10, 3, 295 – 310.

Longman, J., (2012), A Pitch-Perfect Voice for a Team in Need of Fine-Tuning. http://www.nytimes.com/2012/09/03/sports/soccer/pia-sundhage-was-pitch-perfect-voice-for-us-womens-soccer-team.html?_r=0Accessed 27.11.2014.

Mallett, C. & Dickens, S., (2009), Authenticity in formal coach education: Online studies in sports coaching at The University of Queensland. *International Journal of Coaching Science*, 3, 79-90.

Mallett, C., (2010), High Performance Coaches' Careers and Communities, in: Lyle, J. and Cushion, C., eds., *Sports Coaching: Professionalism and Practice*, Elsevier, London, 119-133.

Martindale, R., Collins, D. & Abraham, A., (2007), Effective talent development: The elite coach perspective in UK sport. *Journal of Applied Sport Psychology*, 19, 187-206.

Mikulincer, M., & Shaver, P. R., (2007). Attachment in adulthood: Structure, dynamics, and change, New York: Guilford Press.

Moon, J., (2004), A Handbook of Reflective and Experiential Learning: Theory and Practice. Routledge Falmer, London.

Neil, R., Cropley, B., Wilson, K., & Faull , A. (2013), Exploring the value of reflective practice interventions within applied sport psychology: Case studies with an individual athlete and a team, Sport & Exercise Psychology Review. 9, pp.42-56.

Nelson, L. & Cushion, C., (2006), Coach education, reflection and learning from experience: The case of the national governing body coaching certificate. *The Sport Psychologist*, 20, 172-181.

Nelson, L., Cushion, C. & Potrac, P., (2006), Formal, nonformal and informal coach learning: A holistic conceptualisation. *International Journal of Sports Science & Coaching*, 1, 247-259.

Olusoga, P., Butt, J., Maynard, I. & Hays, K., (2010), Stress and Coping: A study of World Class Coaches, Journal of Applied Sport Psychology, 22, 3, 274-293.

Potrac, P., Brewer, C., Jones, R., Armour, K. & Hoff, J., (2000), Toward an holistic understanding of the coaching process. *Quest*, 52, 186-199.

Potrac, P. & Cassidy, T., (2006), The coach as 'a more capable other'. in Jones, R. (Ed.) *The Sports Coach as Educator*. Abingdon, Routledge.

Santos, Jones, R. & Mesquita, I., (2013), Do coaches orchestrate? The working practices of elite Portuguese coaches, Research Quarterly for Exercise and Sport, 84 (2), 263-72.

Rees, T., Ingledew, D., & Hardy, L., (2005), Attribution in sport psychology: seeking congruence between theory, research and practice, Psychology of Sport and Exercise 6, 189–204.

Ryan, R., & Deci, E., (2000), Self-determination theory and the facilitation of intrinsic motivation, social development, and well-being. *American Psychologist*, 55, 68-78.

Schön, D., (1983), The Reflective Practitioner: How Professionals Think in Action. New York: Basic Books.

Stoszkowski, J. & Collins, D., (2014), Blogs: A Tool to Facilitate Reflection and Community of Practice in Sports Coaching?, The International Sports Coaching Journal, Volume 1, Issue 3, 139-151.

Trudel, P., & Gilbert, W., (2006), Coaching and coach education. In: D. Kirk, M. O'Sullivan & D. McDonald (Eds.), Handbook of physical education (pp. 516–539), London: Sage.

van Manen, M., (1995), On the epistemology of reflective practice. Teachers and Teaching: Theory and Practice, 1 (1), 33-49.

Weiner, B., (1985), An attribution theory of achievement motivation and emotion. Psychological Review, 92, 548–573.

Weiner, B., (1986), An attribution theory of achievement motivation and emotion. New York: Springer.

Weiner, B., (1991), An attributional look at explanatory style. Psychological Inquiry, 2, 43–44.

Weiner, B., Frieze, I., Kukla, A., Reed, L., Rest, S., & Rosenbaum, R. M. (1971), Perceiving the causes of success and failure. Morristown, NJ: General Learning Press.

Williams, S. & Kendall, L., (2007), Perceptions of elite coaches and sports scientists of the research needs for elite coaching practice, Journal of Sports Sciences, 25 (14), 1577-86.

Woitalla, M., (2012), The Role Model Coach: Pia Sundhage. http://www.socceramerica.com/article/47761/the-role-model-coach-pia-sundhage.html Accessed 27.11.2014

Woodward, C., (2005), Winning! The story of England's rise to rugby world cup glory. London: Hodder & Stoughton.